ACT I.
A private sittingroom in the Seaview Hotel, Inish. A July morning.

ACT I1
The same, early evening, ten days later.

ACT III.
The same, a week later, morning.

The First Production of *DRAMA AT INISH* took place in the Abbey on the 6th February, 1933. The cast was as follows :—

JOHN TWOHIG (proprietor of the Seaview Hotel	W. O'Gorman
ANNIE TWOHIG (his wife)	Ann Clery
LIZZIE (his sister)	Christine Hayden
EDDIE TWOHIG (his son)	Joseph Linnane
PETER HURLEY, T.D.	Eric Gorman
CHRISTINE LAMBERT	Gladys Maher
HECTOR DE LA MARE	Paul Farrell
CONSTANCE CONSTANTIA	Elizabeth Potter
HELENA (a servant)	Nora O'Mahony
MICHAEL (the boots)	Rex Mackey
JOHN HEGARTY (a reporter)	Fred Johnson
TOM MOONEY (a Civic Guard) ...	J. Winter
WILLIAM SLATTERY, P.S.I. ...	Don Barry.

Produced by LENNOX ROBINSON

The play was subsequently done in the Ambassador's Theatre, London, and in New York under the title *"Is Life worth Living?"*

For   Dolly

DRAMA AT INISH

An Exaggeration in Three Acts

Po 0223043Z

by

LENNOX ROBINSON

DUBLIN :

JAMES DUFFY & CO., LTD.

1953

Door centre back. Fire, mantlepiece, overmantle down left. Window up right. Table or writing desk down right, side-board right of back door. Table right of centre stage. Sofa up stage of fire. Armchair down stage of fire. Three chairs (two placed at table centre: one down stage of table left). Pouffe at fire. Fender and fire-irons. Pictures, ornaments, etc. Silver ware on sideboard. Small table left of door back. Plant on stand at window. Tray, decanter of whiskey, syphon of soda, glasses (at least six), on side-board. Decanter of port on side-board. Room number-board hanging near table right. Pen, ink, letters, letter rack, stationery cabinet, papers, etc., on table right. Two electric brackets at fire. Hand lamp on table right. Switches at fire-place and at door right.

OFF RIGHT.

Small tray with two cups, two saucers, two spoons. (HELENA).

Book of the Play (HECTOR).

Cigarettes and matches.

DRAMA AT INISH

ACT I.

Inish is a small seaside town in Ireland of not much importance save for the three summer months when it is a point of attraction for people seeking sea breezes and a holiday. It has boarding houses but only one hotel of any size—The Seaview Hotel—owned by MR. JOHN TWOHIG, *who is the most important man in the town, chairman of most of its committees and a genial despot. We are looking at a private sitting-room in the Hotel. A bright, comfortable, unpretentious room, well-worn furniture, perhaps a piano, certainly a side-board ornamented by a fern or an aspidistra. There is a syphon of soda water on the sideboard, half a dozen glasses, a decanter of Port. No fire burns in the grate, for it is a fine summer morning and sunshine is streaming through the window. There is a small table in the middle of the room and a larger table against the wall. This table is littered with letters and bills, and the confusion is being made worse by a middle-aged woman,* MISS TWOHIG, *who is distractedly hunting through the papers. She is a pleasant-looking woman, well dressed but obviously a spinster. After a little ineffectual hunting she goes to the door, opens it and calls:—*

LIZZIE : Helena! Helena! (HELENA *appears: A neat little servant just over twenty*).

HELENA: You called, ma'am—miss, I mean?

LIZZIE : I should think I did call; I've been calling you for the last hour. Where at all have you been?

HELENA : I was getting the hins out into the back yard.

LIZZIE : Why couldn't Michael have done that?

HELENA : Sure Michael's gone to meet the train.

LIZZIE : It can't be that late (*She looks at her watch*). My gracious, it's gone half eleven; the train will be in any minute.

HELENA : It's in already, miss; I heard it puffing and I in the yard.

7

LIZZIE (*in a great fuss*) :   Well now, Helena, we must keep clear cool heads.   There's quite a crowd of people arriving on that train, but there's no need for us to get into a fuss; quite the contrary, quite the contrary.   'Twould be a queer thing if we weren't able to deal in a quiet business-like way with half a dozen or ten guests.

HELENA (*cooly*) :   Yes, miss, to be sure.

LIZZIE :   If ye'd only come the first time I called you—

HELENA :   Sure I was with the hins, miss.

LIZZIE :   I know, I know.   Where's Master Eddie?

HELENA :   Gone to the train, miss.

LIZZIE :   Why so?

HELENA :   I don't know, miss.   He put on his new suit after breakfast, and I heard him telling his pappy he was going to meet the train.

LIZZIE :   Oh, to be sure, to be sure.   Miss Lambert's amongst the arrivals.   Which brings us back to business, Helena.   She'd better have number twelve.

HELENA :   She don't like tnat room, miss; 'tis too noisy.   'Tis number tin she always has.

LIZZIE :   Very well.   Ten for her.   Then there's Mr. Cronin and Mr. Hunt.

HELENA :   The min about the land?

LIZZIE (*with dignity*) :   The gentlemen from the Land Commission. Let them have twelve and thirteen.

HELENA :   Nayther of them will look at thirteen.   Them Commissioners are very suspicious.

LIZZIE :   Dear, dear, what a bother.   Well, give them eleven and twelve.

HELENA :   The master said no one was to go into eleven till he'd have the bed repaired.

LIZZIE :   Well, we'll give them nine and ten.

HELENA :   Sure you've put Miss Lambert into tin.

LIZZIE (*growing more distracted*) :   Good gracious me, what'll we do at all, at all?

HELENA :   'Tis easy enough, miss.   What's wrong with fifteen? To be sure it's a double bed, but Mr. Hunt would be glad of it. Sixteen stone if he's an ounce and . . . .

LIZZIE :   No.   I'm keeping that room for Mr. de la Mare and Miss Constantia.

HELENA (*shocked*) : Mr.—and Miss Constatia! Glory, miss

LIZZIE : It's quite all right, Helena. Actresses they are—I mean she's an actress and so is her—I mean he's an actor and so is—well, anyhow, they're man and wife these years and years. O'Hara or some name like that I believe they are really.

HELENA : I see, miss.

LIZZIE : Where were we at all? Miss Lambert in number twelve—

HELENA : Let you leave it to me, miss, I'll straighten it out. (*She gabbles off*). Mr. Hunt number twelve, Miss Lambert tin, Mr. Cronin fourteen, and the play actors in fifteen.

LIZZIE : I believe there are one or two others coming, but I've lost the bit of paper.

HELENA : It doesn't matter, miss; sure there's lashing of rooms.

LIZZIE : That's a good girl, that's a good girl. But mind, no fuss or excitement, be cool and business like. I suppose the master's gone to the train too?

HELENA : Yis, miss. And the mistress is in her bedroom trying on some dresses came from Dublin by the first post.

LIZZIE : More dresses? And what about the one she got for the races only ten days ago?

HELENA : I know, miss. Stacks of them she has, but she said she'd be out at the theatre every night nearly for the next month.

LIZZIE : Oh yes, of course; I forgot. Ah, here's the first arrival. (*For the doors opens and admits* CHRISTINE LAMBERT *and* EDDIE TWOHIG. CHRISTINE *is a capable looking, handsome young woman of twenty-five: Eddie a nice but rather soft young man a year or two younger.*) Well, Miss Lambert, it's welcome you are. How are you at all, at all?

CHRISTINE (*Letting herself be kissed*) : Good morning, Miss Twohig, how are you? You're looking splendid.

LIZZIE : I can't complain, thank God.

CHRISTINE : And how are you, Helena?

HELENA : Very well, miss.

LIZZIE : It's been a grand summer so far, hasn't it.

CHRISTINE : Yes, indeed, but Dublin has been stifling. I was glad to get out of it.

LIZZIE : I'm sure you were. Ah, well, the sea breezes will soon bring the colour back to your cheeks—not indeed that you're looking pale, but nowadays there's no telling the natural bloom from the false.

CHRISTINE : Oh, Miss Twohig!

LIZZIE : Only my little joke, dear. You mustn't mind me. Sure when you're young you might as well be dead as not be in the fashion. Don't I remember. Helena, run and make Miss Lambert a cup of tea.

CHRISTINE : Please don't bother.

LIZZIE : No bother at all. I always have one myself about this hour to shorten the morning. Hurry, Helena.

HELENA : Yes, miss. (*She goes out*).

CHRISTINE : I had breakfast on the train.

LIZZIE : Sure that's hours ago. What you should have is a cup of tea and a nice little nap and then you'll be in smart shape for your lunch.

CHRISTINE : Indeed no. I must make an appearance at the factory before lunch and let the secretary know I've arrived.

LIZZIE : Ah, let the factory wait. How long will you be staying?

CHRISTINE : Three or four weeks, I suppose. It always takes about that long to get through the factory's accounts.

LIZZIE : That's grand news for Eddie. How well he found out the train you were coming on.

EDDIE (*blushing*) : Ah, go on, Aunt.

CHRISTINE : I wouldn't believe it was Inish station if Eddie wasn't waiting on the platform for me.

LIZZIE : Indeed, but he's the faithful boy. I can tell you, Miss Lambert, there's girls breaking their hearts in Inish for Eddie, but not a look will he look at one of them. No, his heart's stuck up in Dublin.

CHRISTINE : Now Eddie, there's a reputation you're getting.

EDDIE : Ah, go on, Christine.

LIZZIE : While Helena is wetting the tea I'll just slip upstairs and see is your room all right. Poor Helena's willing enough, but no system. We're putting you into number—number—which number at all is it?

CHRISTINE : I'm generally in ten.

LIZZIE : That's it.   Ten, of course.   " Helena," says I, "ten Miss Lambert's accustomed to have and ten she must get."   Well, I'll be back in a few minutes.   I'm leaving you in careful hands. (*She goes out*).

CHRISTINE : It's nice to be back again, Eddie.

EDDIE : Is it?   Do you really mean that?

CHRISTINE : Of course I do.   And it was very nice of you to meet me at the station, and that's a very nice suit you've got on. In fact everything's very nice.

EDDIE : I got it last week for you — I mean, against your coming.

CHRISTINE : That's great extravagance.   Didn't you get one before you came up to Dublin for the Spring Show?

EDDIE : I did.

CHRISTINE (*Teasing*) : I don't believe your Aunt Lizzie is right at all.   I believe you've fallen for that pretty Miss MacCarthy —or would it be for the little Mulcahy girl—Bubbles Mulcahy?

EDDIE : You know that's not true.   I—I'd like to ask you something, Christine.

CHRISTINE : Same old question, Eddie?

EDDIE : Yes.

CHRISTINE : Isn't it a bit soon?   I'm not here an hour yet.

EDDIE : I can't help it.   Have you — have you changed your mind at all?

CHRISTINE : No, Eddie, not at all.   You're a dear nice boy and I'm very fond of you, but I don't want to marry you.

EDDIE : I see.   (*He is depressed for a few seconds but quickly cheers up*).   Well, maybe you'll change your mind.   What about a round of golf this afternoon?

CHRISTINE : Imposs.   You forget I'm down here to work.   After tea, maybe; it's light till nine these evenings.

EDDIE : I'm taking you to the theatre to-night.

CHRISTINE : The Theatre?   The Pavilion?   Oh, Eddie I'm sick of those comic troupes; I don't even get a good laugh out of them. They're very stupid and vulgar.

EDDIE : They're not comics, just you wait and see.   We're running a first-class repertory company this summer.

CHRISTINE : You're what?

EDDIE : Intellectual sort of plays, you know.

CHRISTINE :   You're joking.

EDDIE :   Not at all.   You know how Inish has been going down the last two summers, people going more and more to Shangarry Strand just because the bathing was better, and then the troupe that was here last summer was the limit—too vulgar altogether, real low.

CHRISTINE :   The Comicalities?   Wasn't that what they called themselves?

EDDIE :   Yes.   Anyhow the Monsignor got a lot of complaints about them, so he and Pappy and Peter Hurley the T.D. put their heads together and decided something must be done to improve the tone of the place, and the De La Mare Repertory Company is opening their season to-night.

CHRISTINE :   For goodness' sake.   I don't think I ever heard of them.

EDDIE :   Oh they're very high class, I believe; do nothing but serious stuff; Russian plays and all that sort of thing, just what you like.   I've a pair of season tickets, so we'll go every night.

CHRISTINE :   I'll go to-night certainly to sample them.   What's the play?

EDDIE :   I forget.   There's a handbill in the bar.   I know Wednesday night is " A Doll's House "—I remember that because it's such a funny name; and either Thursday or Friday there's " The Powers of Darkness "—isn't there a play called that?

CHRISTINE :   Yes.   But Inish will never support that sort of stuff.

EDDIE :   We'll give it a try, anyway.   Didn't you see Pappy at the station?

CHRISTINE :   Yes, in the distance, in the middle of a lot of queer-looking people.

EDDIE :   That's them.   I mean that's the Repertory Company. The two principals—Mr. de la Mare and Constance Constantia— are stopping here.   We're putting them up free because, of course, Pappy owns the Pavilion, I suppose they'll be along in a few minutes; they had a deal of baggage to look after.

CHRISTINE :   Well, I think this is most exciting.   I'm sure they'll be more comic than the Comicalities, anyway.

EDDIE :   I was dead keen for them to come.

CHRISTINE : Why Eddie?

EDDIE : I feel very ignorant along with you, Christine. You get books in Dublin and go to plays and things, and I don't get a bit here. I thought these plays would improve my mind like.

CHRISTINE : You've a very nice mind, Eddie—leave it alone.

EDDIE : Ah, no; I'm only a kind of a country lout. You're right to keep on refusing to marry me. But maybe by the end of the summer—

CHRISTINE : Now, now; no more of that. (HELENA *puts her head in, all excitement*).

HELENA : The play-actors are coming, miss. Michael has a truck of luggage—such boxes you never seen, and you're in number tin, miss, in case Miss Twohig makes any mistake.

CHRISTINE : All right, Helena.

HELENA : And I'll be a bit delayed with your tea. (*She goes*).

CHRISTINE : Eddie, I'm feeling quite excited; aren't you?

EDDIE : No.

CHRISTINE : Have you no imagination? Suppose that in another moment that door opens and a ravishing young actress comes in and—

EDDIE : Ssh! (*For the door is opening and admits, first, big genial* JOHN TWOHIG: *He ushers in* CONSTANCE CONSTANTIA *and* HECTOR DE LA MARE. *Goodness knows what age* CONSTANCE *is: Her dyed dark-red hair may make her look older than she is instead of younger, as she hopes. Although it is summer she is wearing a heavy fur coat. Her handbag is an exaggeration. She moves with beautiful grace—but knows she does. She has played so many parts that her face has little character of its own: just now it is made up a little too tragically for a bright summer morning.* HECTOR *is very black in the hair, very black in the clothes, very pale in the face*).

JOHN : Come in, come in. This is the sitting-room I was telling you about, Miss Constantia. It's our private room, but you're welcome to use it.

CONSTANCE : Ah, what a charming room. Isn't it divine, Hector?

JOHN : Oh, Miss Lambert, how are you? You got here before

us. This is Miss Constance Constantia and Mr. Hector de la Mare.

CONSTANCE : How do you do? (*Mutual shaking of hands between the three*).

JOHN : Miss Lambert comes from Dublin; she's with the big firm of accountants in O'Connell Street and she comes down to audit the accounts of our factory twice a year and see we don't make off with the money. She's quite an old friend of ours and that boy of mine is breaking his heart over her.

EDDIE (*blushing as usual*) : Ah, go on, Pappy.

JOHN : Come and shake hands with Miss Constantia, Eddie. Where's your manners?

EDDIE (*shaking hands*) : I'm pleased to meet you.

CONSTANCE : Charmed. (*He shakes hands with Hector.*)

JOHN : Has Eddie been telling you, Miss Lambert, about the plays.

CHRISTINE : Yes, indeed. I think it's a splendid idea. I'm awfully interested.

HECTOR : An experiment, Miss Lambert, an experiment. A seaside audience—to me, I confess, an unknown quantity.

CONSTANCE : You remember, dear, that week in Southsea three years ago.

HECTOR : I had forgotten. We played—?

CONSTANCE : To miserable audiences of ignorant people.

HECTOR : Did we? But I meant, what play?

CONSTANCE : " The Lyons Mail."

HECTOR : Ah, I never quite do myself justice in melodrama. That tour was a mistake—financially and artistically—yes, a financial and artistic mistake.

JOHN : That was a pity, then. But won't you all sit down? There's a comfortable chair, Miss Constance—Miss Constantia, I mean.

CONSTANCE : Thank you. (*They all sit*).

HECTOR : Yes, Miss Lambert, I now confine myself entirely— with the co-operation of Miss Constantia—to psychological and introspective drama. The great plays of Russia, an Ibsen or two, a Strindberg—I think very little of the French.

JOHN : The Monsignor was dead against French plays.

HECTOR : He was perfectly right. The French theatre is superficial; no feeling for the psyche; of the flesh, fleshy.

JOHN : Tch, tch, tch.

HECTOR : The English theatre—

JOHN : We thought, things being the way they are, it was safer to keep off English plays this summer.

HECTOR : You lose but little. Of course there is Shakespeare. (*A reverential little murmur of* " Of Course " *runs round the room.*)

CONSTANCE : My Lady Macbeth—do you remember, Hector, in Dundee?

HECTOR : Perfectly, darling. A most marvellous performance, Miss Lambert.

CHRISTINE : I love Macbeth. The last Lady Macbeth I saw was Mrs. Patrick Campbell's.

CONSTANCE (*with gentle pity*) : Ah, poor Mrs. Pat. Did you like her?

CHRISTINE : Immensely.

CONSTANCE : Really? (LIZZIE *and* ANNIE—MRS. TWOHIG— *come in.* ANNIE *matches her husband, large and genial. Her clothes are a little too smart for that hour in the morning*).

JOHN : Here's my wife. Annie, this is Miss Constantia.

CONSTANCE : How do you do?

JOHN : And my sister, Miss Twohig, (*mutual greetings*), Mr. de la Mare, my wife, my sister (*mutual greetings*). My sister helps me to run the hotel and the shop; it gives my wife more time to be thinking of dresses and fal-lals.

ANNIE : Get away with you, John. Oh, Miss Lambert, dear, I never saw you. How are you?

CHRISTINE (*kissing her*) : Splendid, Mrs. Twohig.

ANNIE : You're looking very smart. That's a dotey little suit you're wearing; where did you get it?

JOHN (*to the others*) : What did I tell you? Clothes all the time.

ANNIE : Wisha, don't mind John. He'd be the last to want me to go around like an old ragbag. Won't you all sit down?

CHRISTINE : I'll just slip up to my room and wash my hands. I'll be down again to have my cup of tea with Miss Twohig. (*She goes to the door.*)

EDDIE : Will I carry your case up?

CHRISTINE : No, Michael will have taken it up, I'm sure. Stay where you are. (*She goes out*).

ANNIE : I think we might all have a little tea.

JOHN (*going to the sideboard*) : I have something here that will do Mr. de la Mare better than tea after his long journey. What about a drop of whiskey, sir?

HECTOR : I rarely touch anything in the daytime, not till after the show, except in the most exceptional circumstances.

JOHN : Well, glory to be goodness, could any day be more exceptional than today—high-class plays in Inish? Come, now, I'll take no denial.

HECTOR : Well, if I must, I must.

LIZZIE : I warn you, Mr. de la Mare, my brother will find some excuse to make every day and every hour of every day exceptional. Helena fills that decanter every morning, and many's the evening we have to send down to the bar for a fresh bottle.

JOHN : Ah, what matter, woman dear. A little drop for you, Miss Constantia?

ANNIE : Nonsence. A nice creamy cup of tea is what Miss Constantia would like. Don't I know?

JOHN : Can't you let her speak for herself?

CONSTANCE : I confess I am partial, occasionally, to a small whiskey and soda.

JOHN : That's the spirit. These women of mine think of nothing but tea, tea, tea all the day long. Bring along the siphon, Eddie.

EDDIE : I have it here, Pappy.

LIZZIE : I hope we'll be able to make you comfortable here, Miss Constantia. If everything's not to your liking you must just come to me. Helena—the servant—is as willing as can be, but flighty; no head on her at all.

CONSTANCE : I am sure we shall be most comfortable.

LIZZIE : This place is quite a home from home—that's what a traveller wrote in our book one day; very clever and terse, don't you think?

CONSTANCE : Oh, quite.

JOHN (*having mixed and handed the drinks*) : Now, Miss Constantia and Mr. de la Mare, here's to your very successful season.

HECTOR : And here is to you, sir, and to Inish. May our visit be profitable to the town—spiritually, I mean.

CONSTANCE : I should like to associate myself with Mr. de la Mare's remarks.

JOHN : Faith, I hope it will be profitable in every way. Them Comicalities last year had me on the brink of ruin.

ANNIE : Indeed they were very low.

HECTOR : I hope, Mr. Twohig, you will not set too much store by material profits. Often, alas, plays of this kind draw very small audiences and make very little money.

JOHN : And why do you go in for them so, if it's not a rude question?

HECTOR : Because, Mr. Twohig, they may revolutionise some person's soul.

ANNIE : Ah, sure, we've had enough of revolutions.

HECTOR : I mean that some young man in the audience may see himself there on the stage, in all his lust, in all his selfishness, in all the cruelty of his youth—a young man such as your son. (*He suddenly swings on* EDDIE *who shrinks away*).

LIZZIE : Is it poor Eddie? There never was a more innocent boy.

HECTOR : I meant nothing personal, (*and now it is* JOHN *who inspires him*). Or some middle-aged man, in all outward appearances respectable, will see himself stripped naked, the sham cloak of virtue torn from his shoulders, and he will stand exposed as the rotten sham he is. (*And now it is* LIZZIE'S *and* ANNIE'S *turn*). Women will see themselves vain, shallow, empty-headed, scheming for power, scheming for husbands, scheming for lovers.

LIZZIE (*awed*) : 'Tis like a mission.

HECTOR : It is a mission, Miss Twohig, a tremendous mission where the pulpit is the stage and the great dramatists preach the sermons. I am myself a convert.

JOHN : Do you mean you used to be a Protestant?

HECTOR : I am not speaking in the strictly religious sense. It happened more than twenty years ago. I was a very young man— in Cork. There used to come to the Opera House once or twice a year a company headed by Octavia Kenmore and her husband in a repertory of Ibsen plays. They played to wretchedly small audiences, and I went every night—to the gallery, for I was very poor. I saw every rotten sham in Cork exposed on that stage. I could translate every play in terms of the South Mall of Montenotte or Sunday's Well. I saw myself on the stage—young puppy that I was—

ANNIE : Ah now, Mr. de la Mara, I am sure you were never that.

HECTOR :   I was.   But those plays changed the current of my life.

JOHN :   And did they change Cork?

HECTOR :   They did not.   We played there two summers ago; the same miserable little audiences of cynical people, the same corruption, public and private.

JOHN :   Ah well, here in Inish we don't think much of Cork. But indeed you'll find us quiet, decent people.   I don't think there's much here to expose at all.   Is there, Annie?

ANNIE :   Sorra a thing.   'Tis too quiet we are: not that I want murders or big crimes or anything of that sort—God forbid—but we're often blue-mouldy for a bit of innocent scandal.   We women can't live without that, you know.   Amn't I right, Miss Constantia?

CONSTANCE :   " To speak no scandal, no, nor listen to it."   Ever my motto, Mrs. Twohig, ever my motto.

LIZZIE :   And a very nice one too, my dear.

ANNIE :   " Always merry and bright."   That was someone's motto, wasn't it?

HECTOR :   That, I believe, is an excerpt from some vulgar musical comedy.   (PETER HURLEY *comes in; an insignificant little mouse of a man*).

JOHN :   Ah, here's me bold Peter.   Mr. de la Mare, I want to introduce our local T.D., Mr. Peter Hurley.

PETER :   How are you?

HECTOR (*shaking his hand very formally*) :   I am honoured to meet you, Mr. Hurley.

JOHN :   And this is Miss Constantia.

PETER :   How are you, miss?   'Morning, Annie; 'morning, Lizzie.

ANNIE :
LIZZIE :   } Good morning, Peter.

JOHN :   What about a drop of whiskey, Peter?

PETER :   Ah, no, thank you, John.

JOHN :   You could chance it, the Dail's not sitting now.

PETER :   Things being the way they are, we might be summoned any minute.

HECTOR :   And may I ask, Mr. Hurley, which party you represent?

JOHN (*who is getting* PETER'S *whiskey*) :   Oh, Peter's a sound Government man.   Aren't you, Peter?   Always on the spot when your vote is wanted. He's not much of a speechifier, Mr. de la Mare, but he's a sound party man. Did you speak in the Dail at all yet, Peter? I don't believe you did.

PETER : I riz twice one day but someone else riz quicker.

HECTOR : They also serve, Mr. Hurly, "they also serve who only stand and wait."

PETER : Thank you, sir.

JOHN : Never mind, Peter, my son, you'll come out strong one of these days. There's a whiskey for you—I won't take " no."

PETER : Thank you, John. Here's to us all.

CONSTANCE (*finishing hers and getting up*) : Perhaps we should be going to the hall, Hector.

HECTOR : I'm afraid Murphy won't have the scene set for another hour.

LIZZIE : And it will be nearly time for your dinner then.

CONSTANCE : And I must rest all the afternoon or I shall be an utter rag.

HECTOR : I'll go down to the hall after dinner and see that everything is all right.

CONSTANCE : Oh, it's not that—it's that scene, the end of the fourth act—I'm so nervous about it.

HECTOR : You're word-perfect, darling.

CONSTANCE : Yes, I have it here (*touching her forehead*), but have I got it here? (*Touching her heart*). Have I, Hector, have I?

HECTOR : I know what you mean. It doesn't vibrate.

CONSTANCE : Or the vibrations are wrong. I don't know, Hector, I don't know. (*She is working herself up very effectively*).

HECTOR : When the moment comes, it will come, right and true.

CONSTANCE : Oh, will it, will it?

HECTOR : It will. Take my hands (*she takes them. They are standing looking into each other's eyes. He clenches her hands in his*). It will.

CONSTANCE (*faintly*) : Thank you, Hector, thank you.

HECTOR : But to make assurance doubly sure, if the company will excuse us we'll retire to our room and go over the scene there.

JOHN :   Certainly, certainly.

LIZZIE :   What is it you want to do?

HECTOR :   Just to run over a short scene that is in the play tonight.   We can do it in our room.

LIZZIE :   With actions?

HECTOR :   With, as you say, actions.   Of course, without props.

ANNIE :   Props?

HECTOR :   Properties.   The correct furniture, the samovar, the little empty cradle.

LIZZIE :   Well, indeed, I've seen that room since all your boxes went up, and between them and the big double bed there's not room, as they say, to swing a cat.   Besides, Helena hasn't the room tidied up yet.

HECTOR :   Dear, dear.

JOHN :   What's the matter with this room?   It's a big airy room, and you're welcome to every bit of it.   Sure when the Temperance Society was putting on " The Coiner " last winter, 'tis here they used to hold their practices.

HECTOR :   But so inconvenient for you all.

JOHN :   Not at all; we can go down to the bar, and I'm sure my wife will want to be showing Lizzie all the grand dresses she got from Dublin this morning.   Come on, all of you.

CONSTANCE :   It seems so cruel to disturb you.

JOHN :   Not another word.   Come along (*There is a general move to the door*).

EDDIE (*low to his father*) :   Pappy.

JOHN :   Well, son?

EDDIE :   Ask them could I stay.

JOHN :   Stay?   Nonsense.

EDDIE :   Ask them, Pappy.

HECTOR :   What is that?

JOHN :   A bit of nonsense of Eddie's.   He wants to stay and hear you.

HECTOR :   No, no, my boy.   Wait for the real thing tonight.

CONSTANCE (*dramatically*) :   Hector, a moment.   He must stay. They all must stay.   I must have an audience.   Even three or four people will make all the difference to me—tell me if I vibrate or if I do not vibrate.   (*She swoops on* ANNIE).   Mrs. Twohig, I implore you, lend me your ears—and your heart.   You are a mother.   I am a mother in this play—an erring one, I admit, but still a mother. I entreat you, stay and hear me.

ANNIE (*kindly*) : To be sure I'll stay if that's the way you feel about it. And Lizzie too, I'm sure.

LIZZIE : I'll wait. Sure me tea is due any minute.

CONSTANCE : Thank you, oh, thank you. Hector, set the stage. (*He considers the room for an instant and decides to have the stage on the side of the room facing the door. He instructs* EDDIE *to move the chairs and the table from the middle of the room. While this is going on*).

PETER (*to* JOHN) : I have to be off. I've to see the Monsignor.

JOHN : Right O, Peter. You'll be at the Pavilion tonight?

PETER : I will, to be sure. (PETER *goes out*).

HECTOR : Will you all sit over here, this side? (*He gets them seated in a little row facing the stage. Constance has taken off her coat and hat and has seized a coloured shawl which had been draping a chair or a sofa and has put it over her head.* HECTOR *gets back into his overcoat and hat and turns up the collar of the coat*). I needn't explain the whole play to you; this is the scene which closes the fourth act. The scene is a poor kitchen in Russia; there is a large Russian stove, a samovar, of course—on this table, (*placing the aspidistra on the table*).

JOHN : A what?

HECTOR : A samovar. Of course you know what that is.

ANNIE (*digging* JOHN *in the ribs*) : Of course.

HECTOR : Miss Constantia's name is Elina; she is a poor servant girl whom I have betrayed earlier in the play. My name is Michael—

JOHN : Have they a name like that in Russia? I thought Michael was a good Irish name.

HECTOR : It is a very common name in Russia.

JOHN : And do they ever shorten it to Mick?

HECTOR : No. Well, she hasn't seen Michael for several years, and in the meantime she has had a baby.

LIZZIE : The creature.

HECTOR : This is the scene of their meeting. Perhaps Master Eddie would hold the book. (*He gives it to him*). The bottom of that page, and don't prompt unless we really dry.

EDDIE (*bewildered*) : Dry?

HECTOR : Fluff. (*Which is just as bewildering*).

CONSTANCE (*sitting in a chair with her foot rocking an imaginary cradle*) : I am rocking a cradle, an empty cradle.

ANNIE : In heaven's name, for what?

HECTOR : Ssh! Ready, Constance?

CONSTANCE : Yes. (*She starts to croon a Russian cradle song*).
> Bala, bala balaika,
> Bala, bala, bala mo.

HECTOR (*coming in stamping his feet and shaking the snow off his coat*) : I am looking for Serge Ilyvitch. I am told he lives here.

CONSTANCE (*not looking at him*) : No one of that name lives here.

HECTOR : But Petro Petrocitch told me—Elina! You?

CONSTANCE (*looking at him now*) : You! Michael!

HECTOR : Yes, it is Michael.

CONSTANCE (*rising slowly*) : Why have you come back, back into my life?

HECTOR : I did not know you were here. You ran away from old Alex.

CONSTANCE : He beat me.

HECTOR : Where did you go?

CONSTANCE : To Moscow, to Niji, to Tobolsk, to—anywhere. (*She sits down again and starts rocking and crooning. HELENA comes in with a small tray and two cups of tea on it. She stands unnoticed in the background listening*).

HECTOR : Why are you rocking a cradle, Elina?

CONSTANCE : Can you ask that, Michael?

HECTOR (*peering at the imaginary cradle*) : But it is empty.

CONSTANCE : Indeed it is empty.

HECTOR : Why is it empty?

CONSTANCE : My baby is dead, our baby is dead.

HECTOR (*slowly covering his face with his hands*) : Our baby? I do not understand.

CONSTANCE : You do understand—betrayer. (*With a great cry*). Michael, Michael, give me back my baby!

HECTOR : Elina— (HELENA *lets the tray fall with a crash. Everyone swings round in surprise*).

ANNIE :

LIZZIE :

        Helena

JOHN :

EDDIE :

HELENA (*echoing* CONSTANCE) :   Michael, Michael, give me back my baby?

LIZZIE :   You're crazed, Helena.

HELENA :   Michael!   Michael!

ANNIE (*rushing io her*) :   'Tis only play-acting, child.

JOHN :   Come now, my girl—(*The door opens and* MICHAEL, *the boots, appears a good-looking honest young fellow*).

MICHAEL :   You were calling?

HELENA (*rushing to him and flinging her arms round his neck*) : Michael, Michael, our baby?

MICHAEL (*trying to disengage himself*) :   Here, hould on—

HELENA :   The baby, the baby.

MICHAEL (*backing out of the room*) :   What baby?

HELENA (*going out with him still clinging to him*) :   Our baby, Michael, Michael.   (*They disappear the words*: " Michael " *and* " Baby " *fade away in the distance*).

JOHN :   Thunder and turf.   Annie, what's the meaning of all this?

ANNIE :   Ah, don't bother me.   (ANNIE *goes out quickly*).

HECTOR :   A highly-strung temperament no doubt.

LIZZIE (*picking up pieces of cups*):   And the lovely tea gone.

EDDIE :   What was she saying, Pappy?

JOHN :   I know no more than yourself.   Just nonsense. (CHRISTINE *comes in*).

CHRISTINE :   Is anything the matter?   I heard shouting.   Oh, is that my tea?

LIZZIE :   That's your tea, Miss Lambert, I'm sorry to say.

EDDIE :   It got spilled, Christine.

CHRISTINE :   Yes, Eddie; I gathered that it had got spilled.

JOHN :   It slipped out of Helena's hand.

CHRISTINE :   I see.   (*She senses that everyone is a little awkward and busy with their own thoughts and is silent*).   I think I'll go down to the factory.

EDDIE :   Will I come with you?

CHRISTINE :   No.   Stay here.   I'll be back in an hour.   (ANNIE *comes in).* I'm going out for an hour, Mrs. Twohig. I won't be late for dinner.

ANNIE *(half listening)* : Yes, dear, Eddie, I'd like you to go and have a walk on the strand for yourself.

EDDIE : Why Mammy?

ANNIE : There's no why. Off with you.

EDDIE : Yes, Mammy.

CHRISTINE : See me to the factory first, Eddie.

EDDIE : Right O— (CHRISTINE *and* EDDIE *go out).*

HECTOR : I apologise, Mrs. Twohig, if anything we did or said has caused a reverberation—

ANNIE : I sent her to her room, but not before she shouted it out in the bar and three men heard her.

JOHN : But in heaven's name what's it all about?

ANNIE : You may as well know; it will be all over the town in an hour. Two years ago—do you remember when I sent Helena to Dublin to have her eyes tested?

LIZZIE : She stayed there four months with your sister, didn't she?

ANNIE : It wasn't her eyes; she had got into a little trouble here and I wasn't going to desert her, a nice little girl like that with no one belonging to her . . . Well, the baby died.

JOHN : Heavens above. I knew nothing of this.

ANNIE : Of course you didn't, nor Lizzie, nor one of you.

JOHN : But—Michael— ?

ANNIE : It was Michael the boots.

JOHN : Michael that's here now.

ANNIE : Of course not. The Michael we had two years ago— don't we call every boots Michael to save trouble, none of them ever staying more than a few months? It was that Michael that hopped off to America with your new suit——d'you remember?

LIZZIE : But she said Michael here.

ANNIE : I know. The playacting turned her head for the moment. It's most unfortunate. God forgive you, Miss Constantia. I'd better go and see after her.

LIZZIE : I'll come with you, Annie. (ANNIE *and* LIZZIE *go out).*

JOHN : Well, well. Imagine her keeping that from me all this time. Aren't women the dickens? And Helena such a nice little girl. I'd better go to the bar and see what's after happening.

(JOHN *goes out.* HECTOR *is about to follow but* CONSTANCE *who has remained rather apart from all this, a little wrapt, stops him*).

CONSTANCE :   Hector.

HECTOR :   Yes, dear?

CONSTANCE :   I am not afraid for tonight.   My vibrations were right.   (*He takes her in his arms and kisses her reverently*).

CURTAIN

ACT II

SCENE I.

(The same scene ten days later. Late afternoon with no sunlight, in fact raining heavily, HECTOR *is seated at the writing table doing accounts.* CONSTANCE *comes in in a mackintosh and hat).*

HECTOR :   Are you going already? Isn't it very early?

CONSTANCE :   I know, but I have some mending to do. I tore my dress at the matinee and I must mend it before the show.

HECTOR :   If things continue as they are going you'll be able to have a dresser next week. Imagine that.

CONSTANCE :   Imagine! I haven't had a dresser for years.

HECTOR :   I've just told Murphy to reserve another row of seats for tonight and till further notice.

CONSTANCE :   Isn't it marvellous?

HECTOR :   It just bears out what I have always said: give people the right stuff, well put on and intelligently acted, and they will support it. I hear there weren't a hundred people in the picture house last night.

CONSTANCE :   Splendid. Oh, those pictures, how I hate them.

HECTOR :   The first three days of this week are fourteen pounds two and threepence better than the first three days last week; we're a clear twenty pounds to the good already; we'll be over forty by the end of the week.

CONSTANCE :   We'll be able to settle O'Byrne's account; he's so odious, threatening us with writs.

HECTOR :   And we can settle with Kelly and Shea and that hotel in Clonmel.

CONSTANCE :   Would there be enough for me to send Mother a little? Poor darling, she's so hard up.

HECTOR :   Of course. Let's send her five pounds. That'll be a nice surprise for her. Oh—and I was thinking of Uncle Bill.

CONSTANCE :   What about him?

26

HECTOR : I thought he might join us. He's a good old character actor.

CONSTANCE : Darling, he's very old, and he does get so very drunk.

HECTOR : I know. But he ought to have a share in our success. After all, he taught me my first stage lessons.

CONSTANCE : Then let's just send him some money.

HECTOR : All right. I will. But you must spend something on yourself, darling.

CONSTANCE : Oh, I want nothing but a few dresses. And what will my boy get for himself?

HECTOR : I was wondering if I could pick up a car cheap—a small one, of course. I believe it would pay for itself very quickly; it would save so much in the way of railway fares.

CONSTANCE : Of course, it would . That's a splendid idea. Oh— and there's May, we forgot May.

HECTOR : So we did. She must get something, of course.

CONSTANCE : Of course. Something really substantial.

HECTOR : We won't have anything left at the end of the week if we're not careful.

CONSTANCE : The bills can all wait; they must. I always think family comes first, don't you?

HECTOR : Undoubtedly. After all, it is we who are making the money, and we have a right to spend it any way we like.

CONSTANCE : Of course. (*She shivers*).

HECTOR : Cold, darling?

CONSTANCE : A little. The weather is depressing, isn't it? If we weren't doing such good business I'd be in the blues.

HECTOR : Strange how the weather broke the day after we opened. Not a gleam of sun since. However, it all helps business.

CONSTANCE : I was wondering whether we couldn't run a children's matineé next week, " Midsummer Night's Dream," or something like that. I could be Titania.

HECTOR : That's an idea. I could play Bottom. (LIZZIE *comes in extricating herself from a wet mackintosh*).

LIZZIE : Oh, Miss Constantia, what an afternoon. I'm dripping. Wouldn't you like a cup of tea?

CONSTANCE : We've had ours, thanks, and I'm just off to the Pavilion.

LIZZIE : I hope you had a good audience this afternoon. I wasn't able to go unfortunately, the hotel takes so much of my time.

CONSTANCE : We had a very good audience.

LIZZIE : I'm glad. What is on tonight?

CONSTANCE : " The Powers of Darkness " again.

LIZZIE : Oh yes, that's where they murder the baby in the cellar. I thought that was a very good one.

HECTOR : An extraordinarily powerful play.

LIZZIE : Yes, indeed. Talking of babies and all that reminds me that the business about Michael and Helena just goes from bad to worse. Annie had a terrible time this afternoon with Michael's mother.

HECTOR : I'm sorry to hear that. What happened?

LIZZIE : It seems the mother drove over from Shangarry Strand in an ass and cart and she gave Annie all sorts; said that her boy's character had been taken away and that the town had no right to be saying—as they *are* saying that there's nothing for poor Michael to do but marry Helena. She blames it all on Annie for calling Michael out of his name—his real name, it seems, is Aloysius—blaming Annie, mind you, who is the best friend the poor girl ever had.

CONSTANCE : That seems very unfair. Ah, it's what always happens; the woman pays, to the uttermost farthing.

LIZZIE (*sighing deeply*) : Yes indeed, it's a troublesome world.

HECTOR : I'm sure you can't have many troubles, Miss Twohig, with your nice home here and your brother and sister-in-law so fond of you and the interest of looking after the hotel.

LIZZIE (*sighing more deeply*) : I don't seem to take any interest in the hotel any more. I don't know what's come to me. Anyway, it's not the same as having a real home of my own.

CONSTANCE (*with soft sympathy*) : Of course it's not. I know.

> *Oh, to have a little house*
> *To own the hearth and stool and all,*

The heaped-up sods upon the fire,
The pile of turf against the wall.
To have a clock with weights and chains,
And pendulum swinging up and down;
A dresser filled with shinging delph,
Speckled and white and blue and brown.

LIZZIE : Exactly, dear. Ah, it takes a woman to understand a woman—if you'll excuse me, Mr. de la Mare. I lay awake all last night thinking of that play by—I never get the name right—it's like a cold in the head.

HECTOR : A cold in the head? I confess—

CONSTANCE : I know who she means, darling. Tchekov, isn't it, Miss Twohig?

LIZZIE : That's it, dear. Tchekov. Do you remember the woman in it? She had her chance and threw it away, and there she was drifting into middle age, alone and neglected, just like myself.

CONSTANCE : You threw away your chance, Miss Twohig?

LIZZIE : I did, dear, I did. If I hadn't been a foolish girl, I'd now be a T.D.'s wife.

HECTOR : No.

LIZZIE : A fact, Mr. de la Mare.

CONSTANCE : Which T.D.?

HECTOR : Hush, Constance. We have no right to prove into an old sorrow.

LIZZIE : It's such an old story that I can talk of it now. Yes, indeed, I might this minute be Mrs. Peter Hurley, T.D.

HECTOR : Dear, dear.

LIZZIE : And my picture in the papers and asked to parties in Dublin and all. And if I cared to, I could dress better than Annie —I've kept my figure better than she did—but what is the use of dressing grand? Sure fine clothes are a poor consolation for a broken heart.

HECTOR : Very true.

CONSTANCE : Why did you throw him over?

LIZZIE : I didn't throw him over, Miss Constantia. Peter Hurley behaved shameful. We were never exactly engaged—thank God, I never gave him the chance to jilt me—but he behaved shameful all the same. He played with my affections, and in the end without so much as by your leave or with your leave took himself off and married a small publican's daughter from the County Clare.

HECTOR : Too bad, too bad. Well, you must remember that " Sorrow's crown of sorrows is remembering happier days." You must be brave, Miss Twohig, and live for the next generation; teach them to see clearer, think straighter, be more fearless.

LIZZIE (*with a sniff*) : I must, I suppose. (ANNIE *comes in and sinks into a chair*).

ANNIE : I'm jaded.

CONSTANCE : Indeed you look worn out, Mrs. Twohig.

ANNIE : Such a day. I never thought I'd live to be called the things that woman called me this afternoon.

HECTOR : Did Mr. Twohig not deal firmly with her?

ANNIE : I never set eyes on John since dinner-time.

LIZZIE : He spent the whole afternoon in the bar.

ANNIE : Did he?

LIZZIE : You'll have to speak to John, Annie; 'tis terrible the way he's drinking.

ANNIE : Ah, not at all.

LIZZIE : Though he's my own brother, I'll have to say it. You're married to a man who's on the high road to becoming a drunkard.

ANNIE : You've no right to say things like that, Lizzie, about your own brother. I hope I see John's faults as clearly as the next, but he is not, never was, and never will be a drunkard.

LIZZIE (*with her usual sigh*) : Well, I only hope you're right.

ANNIE : Everything seems going astray lately, the weather and all.

HECTOR: Except the Pavilion, Mrs. Twohig; don't forget the Pavilion. Though you don't patronise us often, I'm sorry to say.

ANNIE : I don't know why, but I couldn't bring myself to go after the second night. They made such a terrible show-up of things. I remember Lizzie here saying the day you came—you were telling us the sort of plays they were—" 'Tis like a mission." And I suppose it is. Maybe I'm stupid and flighty, but I don't hold with those plays at all—of course, it's only here I'd say such a thing; I'd never breathe a word outside for your sakes and John having the Pavilion. And sure you couldn't wear nice clothes going to that class of play; the best you could do would be a sort of half mourning.

LIZZIE : I couldn't live without those plays. I was mad that I couldn't get to the matineé this afternoon. (MICHAEL *puts his head in the door*).

ANNIE : Am I wanted, Michael?

MICHAEL : You're not, ma'am, but did you hear the terrible thing that's after happening Jim Clancy?

ANNIE : No, what is it?

MICHAEL : Threw himself off the end of the pier.

ANNIE : For pity's sake.

LIZZIE : Dear, dear, dear. (*Everyone rises in concern*).

ANNIE : Was he drowned dead?

MICHAEL : No, ma'am. Bruised. The tide was out.

ANNIE : Thank God.

HECTOR : What was the reason for it?

MICHAEL : No one knows, sir. He kem out of the Pavilion —he'd been watching the play—and he went to the end of the pier and stood there for a bit and then lepped over. The Fehily boys were watching him; 'tis they pulled him out.

CONSTANCE : Only bruised?

MICHAEL : Yes, ma'am; 'tis one of them congested piers, and when the tide is out there's only a sup of water. He must be out of his senses to think he could drown there. Now if he'd gone to the white rocks there'd be some chance for him.

ANNIE : Well, indeed, I'm glad he didn't.

MICHAEL : Well, he's roaring on the bed in the mother's place and saying it's there he will go the next time he has a free minute. The doctor's with him; he says he's sort of melancholy (JOHN's *voice is heard calling* "Michael"). There's the boss calling for me. (MICHAEL *goes out*).

LIZZIE : Ah, it's a sad, sad world.

ANNIE (*sitting down again*) : Everything seems going astray.

HECTOR : Yet it is interesting to find a temperament like that in Inish. We Irish, we're very like the Russians really.

CONSTANCE : Quiet on the surface but with such hidden depths of feeling—like Miss Twohig here.

ANNIE : Is it Lizzie?

HECTOR : Yes. Your sister-in-law has allowed us to know a little of her tragedy.

ANNIE : Her tragedy? What under heaven are you talking about? (JOHN *bursts in. He has some papers in his hand*).

JOHN (*to* ANNIE) : Do you see these?

ANNIE : I do, to be sure.

JOHN : Do you know what they are?

ANNIE : They look like bills.

JOHN : Then they look like what they are—bills, bills, bills. This one from Kelletts, this from Arnotts, these two from shops in Grafton Street. I never heard the names of before. Woman, dear, do you want to ruin me?

ANNIE : I do not.

LIZZIE : You've been drinking, John.

JOHN : I have not, and if I had itself wouldn't I have good reason to try and drown my troubles? Where in heaven's name am I to get money to pay all these?

ANNIE : There can't be so much in them after all.

JOHN : Not so much? Look here—nineteen pounds and eleven-pence. And here—ten pounds nineteen and sixpence, and here—

LIZZIE : It's not very nice to be saying these things before Miss Constantia and Mr. de la Mare.

JOHN : Ah, keep out of this, you.

CONSTANCE : As a matter of fact I'm just going.

HECTOR : So am I.

JOHN : I don't want either of you to go. What I've got to say can be heard by the whole world. I've tried to rear Eddie well and respectable and leave a nice business behind for him, and here's my wife stabbing me in the back all the time, buying a mountain of clothes, hats, ribbons and the like to flaunt around the town.

CONSTANCE : I'm sure Mrs. Twohig becomes them well and does you credit. I think you should be proud of her.

LIZZIE : Indeed he should, Miss Constantia.

JOHN (*to* ANNIE) · You say nothing?

ANNIE : No, but I'm thinking a lot.

JOHN : Slowly my eyes are being opened, and I begin to see what a fool I've been all these years, just making a home for you, making a nest for you, making -a-a-a.

LIZZIE : Making a doll's house for her.

JOHN : Exactly. A doll's house. You took the words out of my mouth. But it has got to stop. If it doesn't, one or the other of us leaves this house.

LIZZIE : John, you wouldn't dream of such a thing.

JOHN : Why wouldn't I? I've my own life to lead, haven't I? I'm not just a blank chequebook, am I? (PETER HURLEY *comes in*).

PETER : I dropped in, John, to say I have to go to Dublin by the evening train. The Dail meets tomorrow.

JOHN : Well, isn't that a pity. You can't be with me to the play tonight?

PETER : No, John, worse luck. Though indeed I think it's a shame the way I'm taking Annie's seat every night.

ANNIE : You're welcome to it, Peter.

PETER : Thank you, Annie. You've been out, Lizzie? (*She looks stonily in front of her*). I was asking had you been out?

LIZZIE : I think, Mr. Hurley, in the future the less conversation you and I have together the better.

PETER : Lizzie. Why so?

LIZZIE : I needn't say.

ANNIE : What ails you, Lizzie?

LIZZIE : Please ask me no questions, Annie; I've said my say.

JOHN : Sure you can't leave it like that and Peter such an old friend of yours.

LIZZIE (*with a sniff*) : Old friends, indeed.

JOHN : Well, isn't he? Didn't you play together as childer?

LIZZIE : Maybe that's what I'm thinking of, and thinking, too, of the way he treated me when I wasn't a child any longer.

PETER : How I treated you?

LIZZIE : Yes, but we'll say no more about it. You can leave me with my thoughts.

PETER : What does she mean, John?

JOHN : I don't know Peter. What's the matter, Lizzie girl? (*But* LIZZIE *won't answer*).

HECTOR : Miss Twohig is, no doubt, thinking of the rather heartless way you behaved long ago.

PETER : Heartless?

HECTOR : Yes, heartless. When you abandoned her—for another.

PETER : I never did anything of the kind. There never was

anything between us except maybe a bit of innocent skylarking now and again.

LIZZIE : Oh, Peter.

CONSTANCE : It may have seemed only skylarking to you, Mr. Hurley, but it broke Miss Twohig's heart.

ANNIE : Did it, Lizzie? I never heard a word of this.

JOHN : Nor I. Such codology was never known. Don't be making an old eejut of yourself, Lizzie.

LIZZIE (*rising with dignity*) : I am sorry I intruded my personal tragedy on you all; I apologise. And now, John, your "old eejut" of a sister will take herself away. (*And she goes out*).

JOHN : Well, can you beat that?

ANNIE : Ah, don't mind her. Did you hear about Jim Clancy?

JOHN : Of course I did. Everyone's talking of it. I'm sorry for the poor boy, and I'm sorry for ourselves too, for there'll be one less in the audience every night, Mr. de la Mare. Jim never missed a performance once.

HECTOR : I see. A real enthusiast.

PETER : But, John, I'm uneasy about Lizzie. It's not in my mind that I've anything to blame myself about, and anyway it was all twenty and more years ago, and we've been the best of friends all along, and she's been a good friend to my wife too.

JOHN : Don't give it a thought, Peter. Some little fancy that came to her. Maybe the weather's accountable for it; I don't feel at all myself this evening.

PETER : I see. Well, I'm off.

JOHN : Will you be staying in Dublin over the week-end?

PETER : Not at all. I'll be home for Saturday. I wouldn't miss the play that night for anything. Goodnight to you all.

EVERYONE : Good night. (PETER *goes out*).

CONSTANCE : I must go too. Hector, are you ready to come?

HECTOR : Yes, I may as well go. (*He goes to the door*). You'll be at the play to-night, Mr. Twohig?

JOHN : Of course.

CONSTANCE (*at the door*) : And Mrs. Twohig?

ANNIE : No, thank you, I'll stay at home and read a magazine I've just bought.

CONSTANCE : Indeed. What magazine is that?

ANNIE (*a little grimly*) : " Comic cuts."

CONSTANCE : Indeed. (*They make a dignified exit not certain whether to be offended or not).*

JOHN : Did you mean that for a slap at them, Annie?

ANNIE : They can take it any way they like.

JOHN : You don't care much about them, I think.

ANNIE : Oh, I suppose they're all right.

JOHN (*trying to make it up*) : Annie; I spoke too sharply to you a while ago and I'm sorry.

ANNIE : You have a right to be. You disgraced me before the whole room.

JOHN : Still, those bills—they were a bit of a slap in the face, coming all by the one post.

ANNIE : I'll see that you're not troubled with any more, I'll never get another dress in Dublin as long as I live; old Peg Murnane can run me up some old skirt and blouse if ever I want a new one— once a year maybe. And I suppose I can sell what I have to some secondhand place and get a few pounds for them, and I'll hand every penny I get to you.

JOHN : Now, now, I don't want you to do anything of the sort. All I'm asking for is a little moderation.

ANNIE : I'm not going to have my own husband telling me I " flaunt " around the town.

JOHN : I shouldn't have said that; I don't know what came to me.

ANNIE : I think I know.

JOHN : The drink? Maybe I had one too many this afternoon.

ANNIE : I wasn't thinking of the drink at all.

JOHN (*getting frightened*): Maybe it's getting a hold of me, like in that play where the man went raving mad and threw a lamp at his wife.

ANNIE : I'd like to see you attempt to throw so much as a spoon at me.

JOHN : And there was that other play—ah, but sure it was vodka they were drinking, not decent Irish.

ANNIE : You take those plays too seriously; sure what are they, only a way of passing an evening.

JOHN : Maybe I do, but they're powerful all the same. Anyway, those same plays are doing well by us. I hear Shangarry Strand is a wash out—of course the bad weather has killed the bathing—but even so we have them bet. The people who have taken houses for the month are fit to be tied because they went there instead of here, and they're having to run two extra buses across here each evening to bring them to the Pavilion. I believe the circus there is empty, and the manager of the Royal Hotel is trying Shakespeare readings in the lounge, but even that won't keep people from dropping over here. We're on the crest of the wave. (EDDIE *comes in: He looks years older. He probably has gone into horn-rimmed glasses. He sits down at the writing table. His parents observe him, and after a pause*). Well, Eddie, son, how's tricks?

EDDIE (*Deep in a book—he has brought two in with him*) :   Oh, all right. (*Pause*).

ANNIE :   Did you get a swim today?

EDDIE: No.

JOHN :   *Too wet, I suppose* (*silence*):   D'je hear about Jim

EDDIE :   No.

EDDIE :   Yes   (*silence*).

JOHN :   Are you coming to the play tonight?

EDDIE :   Of course. (*Silence*)

JOHN :   What's the old book?

EDDIE :   Just a play.

JOHN :   What's it called?

EDDIE :   " The Dance of Death."

JOHN :   Oh. (*Silence: but* ANNIE *tries to makes things pleasanter*).

ANNIE :   When I was Eddie's age I always liked plays with a bit of dancing in them. (*Silence*).

JOHN :   And what's the other book?

EDDIE (*with a murderous look at him*): It's called "Fathers and Children," and it's not a play; it's a novel by Turgenev, and it's about the way the old misunderstand the young and how damnable everything is.

JOHN :   I see. (*There is a dreadful silence.* JOHN *gets up quickly*). I'm going to get my tea. Are you coming, Annie?

ANNIE :   I'll stay for a bit with Eddie. (JOHN *goes out*). What's wrong, Eddie?

EDDIE (*still sullen*) :   Nothing.

ANNIE :   I don't like you being rude to Pappy.

EDDIE :   I wasn't rude. (ANNIE *sighs: gives it up.* CHRISTINE *comes in and* ANNIE *rises with relief*).

ANNIE :   Oh, Miss Lambert, dear, I know you're famished for your tea. It should have been ready half an hour ago, but I can't do anything with Helena these days. I'll go and hurry her up. (*She goes out*: CHRISTINE *sits down rather wearily*).

EDDIE :   Tired, Christine?

CHRISTINE :   Just a bit.   The accounts seemed specially tangled today, and then the weather—doesn't it give you the hump?

EDDIE :   No, it doesn't.   I like it like this.   When you think of the terrible things that go on in the world every day—every day, Christine—it seems as if the sun had no right to shine at all.

CHRISTINE :   That's a dreadful thing to say, Eddie.

EDDIE :   Isn't it the truth?

CHRISTINE :   No, I'm sure it's not.   I think there are lots of lovely things in the world.   Little children, and flowers, and the sea and—and oh, all sorts of things.

EDDIE :   But the children seem to suffer the worst of all, and the flowers die, and the sea wrecks ships, and—

CHRISTINE :   Oh, come off it, Eddie.

EDDIE :   What do you mean?

CHRISTINE :   You'll be giving me the blues next.   What's the matter.   You're looking so solemn the last few days.

EDDIE (*very solemn*) :   Perhaps I'm beginning to realise what life means.

CHRISTINE :   If you know that, you'll know a lot, Eddie—more than the wisest man ever knew.

EDDIE :   I think one learns through suffering.

CHRISTINE (*involuntarily*) :   Good Lord.   Excuse me, Eddie. . . . Tell me, are you ever going to go to work?

EDDIE :   I do work.

CHRISTINE :   Not what I call work.

EDDIE :   Do you want me to go away somewhere; get a job?

CHRISTINE :   Maybe.

EDDIE :   Why should I?   I have this place to walk into some day, I help Pappy in the business, I do quite a lot of work.

CHRISTINE :   That seems—soft.

EDDIE :   I'd like to improve people—or rather help them to improve themselves.

CHRISTINE :   But have you no ambition for yourself?

EDDIE :   There was one time I had.

CHRISTINE :   When was that?

EDDIE :   You know very well.

CHRISTINE : Oh.

EDDIE : You killed it stone dead when you turned me down time after time.

CHRISTINE : I want to live my own life, free and independent, or else marry a husband I can respect—someone who is doing big important work, not a—a—

EDDIE : —son of a country hotel-keeper with a grocery business and a bar at the back of the shop? Go on, say it.

CHRISTINE : You've said it.

EDDIE : Thank you. I can see your point, Christine. You'd never have liked to be my doll, my plaything.

CHRISTINE : No, Eddie, I wouldn't.

EDDIE : You are quite right. But I, too, Christine, have my life, my destiny to work out, my—

CHRISTINE : Oh, Eddie, come off it. Can't you be friendly and nice the way you used to be? Why, we were as jolly as possible the day I arrived last week. Don't you remember?

EDDIE : Maybe I didn't realise—

CHRISTINE : Well, stop realising. Be nice, Eddie.

EDDIE : You've not been so nice to me.

CHRISTINE : I'll try to be.

EDDIE : Well, here it is for the last time. Will you marry me?

CHRISTINE (*wearily*) : Oh, forget it, Eddie.

EDDIE (*with real passion*) : Never, never, as long as I live. Christine, will you marry me?

CHRISTINE : No.

EDDIE (*with dignity*) : Thank you. I am sorry I bothered you. I won't do it again.

CHRISTINE (*trying a little to flirt with him*) : I rather liked being bothered, you know.

EDDIE : Did you? That shows how little you understood. (LIZZIE *comes in in excitement*).

LIZZIE : Miss Lambert, you're a woman of the world; what's a suicide pact?

CHRISTINA : Good heavens. Surely you weren't thinking—what are you talking about?

LIZZIE : Tom Mooney of the Gardai has been telling me—it's all over the town—a young couple at Shangarry Strand turned the gas on and left a bit of a note, posted it to the girl's mother in fact, saying 'twas a suicide pact; but sure it was a penny in the slot meter and it gev out, and I suppose the young couple thought better of it, or maybe they had no change in the house; anyway, they're alive and little the worse of it.

CHRISTINE : What a wonderful escape. Who were they? (ANNIE *comes in*).

LIZZIE : The young fellow had a job shifting scenery with Mr. de la Mara and the wife sold chocolates in the theatre. They'd come and go by the bus every day to Shangarry. The man was dismissed last Saturday because he'd be all night with his eyes and ears glued to some crack in the scenery listening to the plays and never doing a tap of work; but he came back every night this week, and the girl used to smuggle him into the back of the pit. It must be on the head of losing his job that he tried to destroy himself.

ANNIE : There's some queer madness in the air. Everyone's behaving strange and different.

EDDIE (*with sincere passion*) : Why should you think them mad? Mightn't what they were going to do be the most sensible thing in the world? To kiss—and die.

ANNIE : Eddie, that's wicked, shameful talk. Where's your religion—and your common sense?

EDDIE : Oh, common sense be hanged. Is life worth living?

LIZZIE : I don't hold with suicides, Annie; I never did. But in a way, Eddie's right. There are times when we all feel that life is not worth living.

ANNIE : I never felt that way, thank God. Did you, Miss Lambert?

CHRISTINE : Eddie has just got a bad touch of growing pains, Mrs. Twohig. I wouldn't take him too seriously.

EDDIE : That's right; throw my youth in my face.

CHRISTINE : I didn't mean to do anything of the kind, Eddie.

EDDIE : You've always treated me as a child and Mammy has too. Well, I'd have you know I'm no longer a child.

ANNIE (*soothing*) : Of course you're not, son.

EDDIE (*rising*) : And I'd have you know that I've just asked Christine for the last time if she'll marry me, and she's said " no," so that's finished—forever. And let you and Pappy stop making jokes about me and her, or I'll—well, I'll do something anyway that will make you sorry. (*He bangs out of the room*).

ANNIE : Wisha, the poor boy. (*She looks appealingly at* CHRISTINE). Miss Lambert, dear?

CHRISTINE : I'm afraid it's no use, Mrs. Twohig. I'm very fond of Eddie, but that's as far as it goes.

LIZZIE : Poor Eddie. I know what he's going through, I know.

ANNIE (*sharply*) : Lizzie, don't be a fool.

LIZZIE (*with a little tragic laugh*) : Ah, that's what they'll call us, Eddie—fools, fools.

ANNIE : Glory be to goodness, I think you're astray in the head too. Come on, Miss Lambert, dear, till I get you your tea (ANNIE *and* CHRISTINE *go out. A thunder shower must be coming up for since* CHRISTINE'S *entrance the room has grown very persceptibly darker.* LIZZIE *sits in the shadows happily sighing to herself*).

LIZZIE : Poor Eddie and poor me! Ah, Peter, Peter!

CURTAIN.

SCENE II.

(The scene is the same as before. The table is laid for supper for two. The standing lamp at the desk is lit. The time is about eleven o'clock at night. CONSTANCE *comes in followed by* HECTOR. CONSTANCE *goes to the fireplace, throws her wrap on the armchair and then lights the brackets at the fireplace.* HECTOR *is at the table).*

HECTOR :   Cold beef again.

CONSTANCE :   Any pickles?

HECTOR :   Only onions.

CONSTANCE : How odious.

HECTOR *(pouring himself a whiskey)*: I have quite made up my mind; that scene at the end of the third act must go.

CONSTANCE :   My scene with Petro Petrovitch?

HECTOR :   Yes. It is unnecessary; the act ceases with my exit. The rest is sheer padding.

CONSTANCE *(nastily)* :   Strange how the audience responds to the " padding "—and your exit never gets a hand.

HECTOR :   Because you deliberately kill it by making that move.

CONSTANCE :   I have to move then. I shall continue to make that move and I shall continue to play that scene. Hector, if you cut that scene, I shall refuse to play.

LIZZIE *(enters)* :   Oh, here you are. I'm trying to get your supper right for you.

HECTOR :   Where's Helena?   *(He pronounces the name in a classical manner).*

LIZZIE :   Helena is incapable with the toothache. Eddie's been out of the house since six—he hasn't been at the play—Annie's gone to bed in tears and John stumped up to his room the minute he got back from the Pavilion. The whole house is on my shoulders.

CONSTANCE :   Poor Miss Twohig.

HECTOR *(looking at the table)* :   Dear, dear. Well, you seem to have got together a very appetising little supper, Miss Twohig.

LIZZIE :   I hope everything will be to your liking.

CONSTANCE *(sitting)* :   I'm too tired to eat anything.

HECTOR :   You must keep up your strength, darling.

CONSTANCE :   I suppose I must (*She drinks*). Pass me the onions Hector.

HECTOR (*passing the onions*) :   Darling. A little bread?

LIZZIE :   What sort was the audience tonight.

HECTOR :   Deplorable. I don't think there were thirty people in the hall. The whole town was looking at the fire.

CONSTANCE (*bitterly*) :   Imagine people looking at an ordinary little fire when they might have been watching a masterpiece.

LIZZIE :   I'll have to admit I slipped out to have a look at the fire myself.

HECTOR :   And remember, darling, it was not quite an ordinary fire. I am told that Mr. Maloney is suspected of having set fire to his shop himself, and is likely to be arrested on the charge of incendiarism.

LIZZIE :   Poor Tim Maloney. As honest a man as ever breathed.

HECTOR :   Of course it's only a suspicion. But ah, Miss Twohig, what depths and what depths there are in people's character.

LIZZIE :   I know, I know. There's my tragedy—

HECTOR :   Exactly. Is there any cheese?

LIZZIE :   I'm sorry to say we're run out of cheese.

HECTOR :   No matter. Will you eat nothing yourself?

LIZZIE :   Ah, no thanks. Anything I took at this hour of night would prey on my stomach. It amazes me to see Miss Constantia able to eat so heartily.

CONSTANCE (*her mouth full*) :   I've taken the merest mouthfull.

LIZZIE :   You're welcome to everything, dear. Well, I must leave you for a few minutes. I must see is everything locked up downstairs. As I told you, the entire house is on my shoulders tonight. (*She starts to go, meeting* MICHAEL *in the door*). What is it, Michael?

MICHAEL :   Nothing, miss.

LIZZIE :   Sure it must be something.

MICHAEL :   'Tis a kind of message I have for Mr. de la Mare.

LIZZIE :   Well, out with it. (MICHAEL *hesitates*).

HECTOR :   What is it, my boy?

MICHAEL :   'Tis sort of private.

LIZZIE :   Oh, more troubles and mysteries. What's the world coming to when the boots as good as tells me to leave the room? I'm bothered out of my life. (*She leaves the room angrily*).

CONSTANCE :   And what is the message, Michael?

MICHAEL :   'Tisn't exactly a message, ma,am.

HECTOR :   No?

MICHAEL :   But I couldn't say what I have to say before the ould one.

HECTOR :   The old one?

MICHAEL :   Ould Lizzie Twohig.

CONSTANCE :   Not a respectful way to talk of your master's sister.

MICHAEL :   Ah, what matter?   I was wondering, sir—At school I was always grand at recitations—

HECTOR :   Yes.

MICHAEL :   I want to be an actor, sir.

CONSTANCE :   Michael.

HECTOR :   An actor!   You?

MICHAEL :   Yes, sir.

HECTOR :   No, no, my poor boy.   Any profession save that.

MICHAEL :   Why so?

HECTOR :   I think if I had my life to live again I'd rather be the boots in the Seaview Hotel than Hector de la Mare.

CONSTANCE :   Hector.

MICHAEL :   Is it you, the boots?

HECTOR :   Yes.

MICHAEL :   You don't know what you're talking about.   Do you know the kind of life I lead?   Up every morning at half six; cleaning knives, cleaning boots, knocking up commercial travellers out of their beds—powerful sleepers every one of them; rousing Helena to get their breakfast; carting their grips to the early train; snatching a bite of breakfast myself, God knows when; feeding the hins and the brood sow; doing a bit of odd gardening; meeting every train that comes and goes; serving in the shop; carrying coals and whiskey up here; never seeing my own bed till midnight or later— ah, get along with you, sir.

HECTOR :   Even so, it would be better than—

MICHAEL :   Now, if I was the like of you, I'd be travelilng the length and breadth of Ireland, maybe England, maybe the whole wide world itself .   I'd be speaking grand speeches and wearing fine clothes. I'd be having people frozen cold in their seats with the terror I'd put on them—the way you stiffened myself out the other night.   Or I'd have them rocking themselves sick with the laughing— not indeed that you are much of a comic, Mr. de la Mare.   I'd be leaving a name after me that would be remembered through the land. I'd not just be " Michael the Boots at the Seaview "—and even the same Michael not being my christened name at all.

CONSTANCE (*touched*) : I shall always call you Aloysius in the future, Michael.

MICHAEL : Thank you, ma'am.

HECTOR : You'd like to give up your nice place here and your kind master and mistress to drag from one small town to another, playing in small halls and dirty little theatres, staying in frowsy lodgings; with no home, no permanent abiding-place; seeing yourself getting older and shabbier every year—

CONSTANCE : Hector, what are you saying?

HECTOR (*almost hysterically seeing himself for a moment as he really is*) : It's true, Constance, it's true; you know it is. Saying to myself, " Shall I ever get a chance? Must it always be the smalls of England and Ireland for me? Oh, my God, to play in a great theatre, thousands hanging on every word I uttered——"

MICHAEL (*fired*) : That's it, sir, that's it. I know sir. But if you'd only hear me recite.

HECTOR : No. No.

MICHAEL : Please, sir.

CONSTANCE : Let him, dear. It can do no harm.

HECTOR : Very well, proceed.

MICHAEL : What'll I do? A comic or a serious.

HECTOR : I should prefer something serious.

MICHAEL (*after thinking a little*) : Well, I learned this after I left school. It wasn't in the reading-book, but I took a fancy to it. I'm told it was written by a man who walked off one day and was never heard of again. 'Tis called " Ballyvourney " which is a place in the mountains of County Cork and a great place for the Gaelic. (*He recites the poem with a serious, simple intensity*).

He came from Ballyvourney and we called him " Ballyvourney,"
   The sweetest name in Erin that we know,

And they tell me he has taken now the last, the last long journey,
   And it's young he is, it's young he is so very far to go.
Before our eyes, just like a flower, we saw his life unfolding,
   As day by day he grew in bloom in early manhood's grace:

> *Ah, Death, to pluck the flower and to snatch from our beholding*
>   *The head of rippled gold and the happy morning face."*

Sure that's a sad ould poem.   Maybe you'd like this better   (*He rattles off, half-singing, half reciting*).

> *While going the road to sweet Athy,*
>   *Hurroo—Hurroo—*
> *While going the road to sweet Athy,*
>   *Hurroo—Hurroo—*
> *While going the road to sweet Athy,*
>   *A stick in my hand and a drop in my eye,*
> *A doleful damsel I heard cry,*
>   *" Och, Johnny, I hardly knew ye.*
> *With drums and guns and guns and drums*
>   *The enemy nearly slew ye,*
> *My darling dear, you look so queer,*
>   *Och, Johnny, I hardly knew ye."*

LIZZIE (*who has come in at the last part of the verse*) :   In the name of goodness, what are you doing, Michael?

MICHAEL (*abashed*) :   Nothing, miss.

LIZZIE :   Nothing?   Nonsense.   Off to bed with you.   You were shocking late getting up this morning.

MICHAEL :   Yes, miss.   Good night to you all.

CONSTANCE ⎫
HECTOR ⎭ :   Good night. (MICHAEL *exits*).

LIZZIE :   You shouldn't let him be bothering you with his capers, Miss Constantia.

CONSTANCE :   I like Aloysius.

LIZZIE :   Aloy—who?   Oh, Michael, you mean?

HECTOR :   You may have something of a genius there, Miss Twohig.

LIZZIE :   Ah, nonsense.   No genius ever could come out of a backward place like Shangarry Strand—or Inish itself, for that matter.

HECTOR :   " It bloweth where it listeth—" (*Rising*).   Well, well, I think I shall retire.   I have had a very pleasant supper, Miss Twohig, and for that, many thanks.   Are you for bed, Constance.

CONSTANCE (*rising*) :   Yes, indeed, I'm worn out.   Good night, Miss Twohig.

LIZZIE :   Good night, dear.

HECTOR :   Good night, Miss Twohig.   (*The two go out.   LIZZIE does a little tidying up at the table and switches off the lights at the fireplace.* EDDIE *enters. He looks more gloomy and distraught than ever).*

LIZZIE : Oh, Eddie, darling, you're back, I was worried about you the whole evening. Where were you?

EDDIE : Just walking and walking and walking.

LIZZIE : I know. You wanted to be alone with your thoughts.

EDDIE : Yes. It's foolish of me, I suppose.

LIZZIE (*sits*) : Foolish? That's what they call us, Eddie, foolish. 'Tis little they understand.

EDDIE : I'll take my books and go to bed.

LIZZIE : Before you go let you sit down for a minute. I want to talk to you.

EDDIE : What is it? (*sitting*).

LIZZIE : Ah, no—sit here—at my feet.

EDDIE (*sitting at her feet*) : We're like the aunt and the nephew in that play on Monday night.

LIZZIE : Aren't we? Eddie, I'd like to tell you the story of my life.

EDDIE : And I'd like to tell you about myself, Aunt Lizzie.

LIZZIE : You see, Peter and I knew each other from the time we were little children.

EDDIE : I was grown up when I first met Christine.

LIZZIE : We lived next door to each other, and we saw one another every day of our young lives.

EDDIE : I'd never see Christine only twice a year, unless I chanced to go to Dublin.

LIZZIE : He had an elder brother that everyone was struck on but I could see nothing in him. It was Peter for me always.

EDDIE : When I first met Christine, Aunt Lizzie, it was like— like—.

LIZZIE (*with a touch of impatience*) : Wait till I tell you about Peter.

EDDIE : It was like sunshine in a dark cellar. (*They now speak together paying no attention to what the other is saying. Entirely engrossed in making pretty, untrue pictures for themselves).*

LIZZIE : He was a year or two older than I was, a bright, curley-headed boy. There was another boy—Jack Murnane—terribly gone on me, but Peter beat him one day, and after that he kept away from me. He'd bring me flowers and sweets, and he called me his little sweetheart. And as we grew older he learned to love me with a man"s love, and one day he wanted to buy me a ring, but I wouldn't let him. He was afraid of his mother, and I think it was she who drove Peter from me—

EDDIE : It was only two years ago, but it seems to me as if I had never lived until she came to Inish. I'd never cared about a girl in my life, only Katie Walsh and one or two others, and that was only to pass the time. I loved her from the minute I set eyes on her, but I was always a bit afraid of her. I was like a dog; she could whistle and I'd come to her. I've always kept a handkerchief she dropped one time; it's in the press in my room and sometimes I sleep with it under my pillow. I've never kissed her. I wouldn't dare. . . .

(*Somewhere about here the Curtain mercifully falls*).

ACT III

(SCENE: *The same a week later. Morning: dull, raining slightly.*
LIZZIE *comes in, ushering* MR. HEGARTY, *a young man*).

LIZZIE : Will you come in here, Mr. ——, Mr. ——

HEGARTY : Hegarty, John Hegarty.

LIZZIE : Oh, yes, you told me, of course. Will you sit down
Mr. Hegarty? I'm afraid my brother is out and my sister-in-law
too; they went out after breakfast and I haven't seen them since.

HEGARTY : That doesn't matter at all, Miss Twohig. I am sure
you can give me all the information I want.

LIZZIE : Well, of course I can tell you about the hotel, seeing
that I more or less run it. I can let you have a very nice room
from about ——

HEGARTY : No, no . I'm afraid I'm not staying. I just want a
little information.

LIZZIE : Information?

HEGARTY : I always think that in these little country towns there's
no place like the hotel for gathering news. The hotel is the hub
of the town, so to speak.

LIZZIE : Maybe.

HEGARTY (*suddenly and dramatically*) : Miss Twohig, why has
Inish suddenly put itself on the map of Ireland?

LIZZIE : Sure it was always there—on big maps, anyway.

HEGARTY : Why has Inish suddenly become news? Not yet
front page news, but front page news maybe to-morrow.

LIZZIE : Front page? Oh, you're from a newspaper?

HEGARTY : I thought I had explained that. I'm not from any
particular paper, I'm free-lance. It's part of my business to read
all the Irish papers every day, and during the last two weeks one
word has caught my eye again and again. Inish! Attempted
suicide at Inish. Boy breaks open till in Inish. Respectable butcher
called McClusky beats up his wife at Inish. Young couple attempt
suicide pact, couple employed at Inish . Now I happen to know Inish.
My sister and I spent a month here two summers ago, for our sins.

48

It was very expensive, and it was deadly dull.

Lizzie : Where did you stay?

Hegarty : Not here. You were even more expensive . But that's not the point. The point is that during that month nothing happened. There wasn't even a decent dog-fight, and now all these things happen—in ten days. An outbreak of this kind doesn't come by chance. I've been putting two and two together—I believe I'm the first journalist in Ireland to put this particular two and two together and I'm here this morning to try and find out what they make.

Lizzie : I don't understand all you say, but sure there was nothing at the back of that boy breaking into McGarry's till except that he wanted money to go to the theatre. McGarry let him off, and Mr. de la Mare gave him a season ticket, and there's been no more about it.

Hegarty : Yes, I hardly expected there was anything in that particular incident, but I've been all round the town this morning— I came from Dublin by the early train—I've been into shops and pubs, and I notice the strangest kind of attitude in the people. Everyone seems suspicious, watching everyone else, expecting something strange to happen. If you mention anyone to anyone else, you're met with a kind of veiled suggestion that they are not what they seem to be; that they have a shady past and are likely to have a blacker future. I hasten to add that no one has had a word to say aga'nst you, Miss Twohig.

Lizzie : Did you mention my name?

Hegarty : I don't think I did.

Lizzie : Well, let you try mentioning it and see what happens. You're right, Mr. Hegarty; this town is full of gossipers and slanderers, and I could tell you things about some of them that would make your hair stand on end.

Hegarty : But they weren't like this two years ago. They just seemed nice, ordinary people, a little on the dull side. Come, Miss Twohig, there's something at the back of it all. What is it?

Lizzie : Indeed, I couldn't tell you—unless it would be the weather. Rain every day for a fortnight.

Hegarty : If rain were accountable for crime, all Ireland would have murdered itself long ago. No, no, it can't be the weather.

LIZZIE : Maybe it's politics. Them and the weather are about the only things we think of outside our own business.

HEGARTY : Yes, I hadn't thought of politics. It might be a curious result of recent legislation. Perhaps your local T.D. could help to elucidate this point.

LIZZIE : Is it Peter Hurley?

HEGARTY : Yes.

LIZZIE : You'd do well not to go near Peter Hurley; he's the deceiver if ever there was one.

HEGARTY : In what way?

LIZZIE : I'd rather not say; it's a personal matter. But be deceitful in one way and you'll be deceitful in every way. Isn't that right, Mr. Hegarty?

HEGARTY : I suppose so.

LIZZIE : Anyway, you can't see him to-day because he's away in Dublin at the Dail.

HEGARTY : Oh, yes, of course. They were having a very important all-night sitting last night.

LIZZIE (*laughing*) : Imagine poor old Ireland depending on the votes of men like Peter Hurley. I have to laugh.

HEGARTY : The division was likely to be very close, I believe.

LIZZIE : Oh, they can depend on Peter. Peter'll vote the way he is told to vote. The creature hasn't the courage of a mouse. (HECTOR *and* CONSTANCE *come in. They look rather gloomy*). Oh, come in, come in; this is a young gentleman from a newspaper— Mr. de la Mare and Miss Constantia—Mr. Hegarty. (*Mutual greetings. Everyone sits down*).

HECTOR : You wanted to interview me?

HEGARTY : Well—er—I'm not sure.

HECTOR : Or perhaps it was Miss Constantia you wanted to talk to?

CONSTANCE : No, please, Hector; you know how I hate publicity and all my pictures are at the theatre.

HECTOR : There are times, darling, when one must sacrifice oneself to the great hungry public.

HEGARTY : I am just looking for general information.

HECTOR : Well, we opened our season here nearly three weeks ago, and we have had the most—I won't say astonishing, because I have always believed that the public at heart—*au fond*, as the French say—is quite sound and wants the best. Fine plays, well presented, mind you, and with suitable *decor* is not at present all it might be. You can understand, Mr. Hegarty, how the exigencies of continual touring ——

HEGARTY (*light breaking on him*) : Oh, you're actors?

HECTOR (*with exaggerated humility*) : Well, I hope we are actors. Are we, Constance, my love?

LIZZIE : The De la Mare Repertory Company, Mr. Hegarty. (*To* HECTOR) Mr. Hegarty is from Dublin, and he's maybe a bit out of touch with things, you must forgive him.

HECTOR : I quite understand and there is nothing to forgive. We have not played Dublin for years. When were we there last, darling?

CONSTANCE : I really can't remember.

HEGARTY : What theatre did you play in?

HECTOR : One of the big ones, of course; I can't remember which.

HEGARTY : And you're doing well here?

HECTOR : We have been doing extraordinarily well—up to this week. Miss Twohig, can you explain the curious falling off in the audiences this week?

LIZZIE : I can not. And I don't know why everyone this morning is asking me to explain everything.

HECTOR : I'm sure the repetory was varied enough—some new plays and some old favourites, but no one comes—at least only a handful. Things seem to be happening in the town all the time, and everybody is so busy talking about what has just happened or waiting for the next thing to happen to have any inclination or time to come to the Pavilion.

HEGARTY : Ah, so you've noticed it too?

HECTOR : Noticed what?

HEGARTY : The accumulation of incidents of a mildly criminal nature.

HECTOR : Oh, there have been many strange things which have not got into the papers.

HEGARTY : It's extraordinarily interesting.

CONSTANCE : It's extraordinarily distressing, Mr. Hegarty, when as a consequence we play to empty houses.

HECTOR : Never mind, dearest. We've learned to take the rough with the smooth.

CONSTANCE : We have. " 'Tis not in mortals to command success, but we'll do more, Sempronius, we'll deserve it."

HECTOR (*chiming in*) : We'll deserve it."

HEGARTY : Bravo !

LIZZIE : I wish you could see some of their plays, Mr. Hegarty. They're gorgeous—though sometimes it's a bit hard to get to sleep after them. That one, Mr. de la Mare, where you throw the lamp at Miss Constantia and are then put in a strait waistcoat—that was a very good one, but of course my favourite is where the baby is murdered in the cellar.

HECTOR : Perhaps you will come to the theatre to-night, Mr. Hegarty. Any representative of the press is, of course, more than welcome.

HEGARTY : I am afraid I have to get back to Dublin.

HECTOR : Well, shall you be here for a little time?

HEGARTY : I think so. At any rate I'll be knocking around the town until the afternoon train.

HECTOR : I see. . . . . I thought, Constance, we might stroll to the Pavilion and look for letters, and if we chanced to come on any photographs, Mr. Hegarty might like to have them. Just as a little souvenir, Mr. Hegarty; just as a little souvenir.

HEGARTY : Thank you very much.

HECTOR (*rising*) : We won't be more than a few minutes. The Pavilion is just round the corner. Will you come, Constance.

CONSTANCE (*rising*) : Yes, I should like a walk. I want to feel the sea-spray beating on my face.

LIZZIE : I'm afraid it's quite calm this morning, dear. The sun was trying to come out a little while ago.

CONSTANCE : What matter? I shall at least get a breath of ozone.

HECTOR : Shall I reserve your seat as usual, Miss Twohig?

LIZZIE (*sadly*) : No, I can't come to-night.

HECTOR : You've missed every night this week. Fie, fie !

LIZZIE : No one is sorrier than myself. But I don't like the way Eddie is going on at all and I want to keep an eye on him.

HECTOR : Dear, dear.

CONSTANCE : What's the matter with Eddie, Miss Twohig?

LIZZIE : Haven't you noticed him yourself? So dark and shut up in himself. And, worse than that, he's broken his pledge. I feel quite frightened.

HECTOR : Where is he?

LIZZIE : I don't know. He's not around the house. I'm sorry, Mr. de la Mare, but I must stay at home to-night.

HECTOR : That's quite all right, Miss Twohig, quite all right. Constance, let us go. (*They go out*).

HEGARTY (*very keen*) : Who is " Eddie " Miss Twohig?

LIZZIE : My brother's only child.

HEGARTY : And he's behaving queerly?

LIZZIE : He is indeed.

HEGARTY : I'd like to speak to him.

LIZZIE : He's out, as you heard me say; but indeed you'll get nothing from him. I'm the only one he speaks to—whenever he does speak—I'm the only one knows what's preying on his mind.

HEGARTY : And what is that?

LIZZIE : The old story, Mr. Hegarty, the old, old story—love's young dream, as Thomas Moore said long ago. Are you married, Mr. Hegarty?

HEGARTY (*rather taken aback*) : Why—yes.

LIZZIE : And happy?

HEGARTY : Very happy.

LIZZIE (*disappointed but making the best of it*) : Ah, you're one of the few lucky ones so. (*A tap at the door*). Come in. (*Enter* SLATTERY *furtive and poorly dressed*). Oh, good morning Mr. Slattery.

SLATTERY : Good morning, Miss Twohig.

LIZZIE : My brother is out, but can I do anything for you?

SLATTERY : You're just the one that can. (*From under his coat he produces a large tin*). D'ye see that?

LIZZIE : I do.

SLATTERY : 'Tis a grand weed killer you sold to Mick Tobin a few years back. I want one the like of it, and they told me below in the shop it's you had the key of all the poisons.

LIZZIE (*taking tin and looking at it*) : So I have . . . . " Kill-em-Quick "—ah, Mr. Slattery, isn't it a pity, we're not allowed to stock that any longer; 'twas too poisonous altogether.

SLATTERY (*very dejected*) : Is that so? Well, have you anything in the nature of rat poison?

LIZZIE : I have, to be sure

SLATTERY : Can I buy some.

LIZZIE : Lashin's of it. Wait till I get me keys.

HEGARTY : Just a minute, Mr. Slattery—pardon my butting in —but what do you want the weed killer for?

SLATTERY : For me weeds.

LIZZIE : Of course.

HEGARTY : And, failing the weed killer, you want rat poison?

SLATTERY : For me rats.

LIZZIE: Of course.

HEGARTY : I see. . . . (*He takes up the tin and examines it thoughtfully*). I imagine, Mr. Slattery, that you are very unhappily married. (SLATTERY *gapes*).

LIZZIE : Sure the poor man's not married at all.

HEGARTY (*taken aback*) : Oh !

LIZZIE : He lives with an old termagant of an aunt who is rotten with money and won't let him have more than sixpence a week in his pocket—pardon me saying so, Mr. Slattery.

SLATTERY : It's no more than the truth.

HEGARTY : But you'll come into all her money when she dies?

SLATTERY : I suppose I will.

HEGARTY : Hm. Very interesting.

LIZZIE : I'll have me keys in a minute.

SLATTERY (*trying to take back the tin*) : Maybe I won't mind to-day. I'll get a few penn'orth of sweets instead.

LIZZIE : No trouble at all.

HEGARTY (*holding on to the tin*) : I think I'll keep this.

SLATTERY (*snatching it from him*) : You will not. (*Very rapidly and noiselessly he leaves the room*).

LIZZIE (*turning; she hadn't seen him go*) : I can't find—oh! he's gone. Isn't that very queer now?

HEGARTY : Very queer, Miss Twohig. I think I've put that two and two together anyhow. This may be a case for the police.

LIZZIE : The police. (*And immediately the door opens and* MOONEY, *a Civic Guard, appears*). Oh! heaven protect us.

MOONEY : Morning, Miss Twohig. Is your brother about?

LIZZIE : He's not.

MOONEY : Or the mistress?

LIZZIE : She's out too. Why do you want them? Can I do anything for you?

MOONEY : Well—I wanted to prepare them like.

LIZZIE : Prepare them?

MOONEY : Break the news, as you might say.

LIZZIE : Merciful heavens, what's happened?

MOONEY : It's Master Eddie.

LIZZIE : Eddie! Eddie! He's dead?

MOONEY : No, no, miss. But he's terrible wet.

LIZZIE : Wet?

MOONEY : Yes, miss. He was in the sea.

LIZZIE : Bathing?

MOONEY : No miss. In his clothes.

LIZZIE : Is he after falling in. Poor little Eddie.

MOONEY : No one knows rightly how he got into the sea, miss.

LIZZIE : And who rescued him?

MOONEY : He rescued himself, miss. It seems he got out of the sea at the White Rocks . Maybe he fell in, or maybe he—no matter. Anyway, he walked out of the sea himself, and then he hid among the rocks because he was ashamed-like to walk through the town dripping wet; but a lad came on home and brought him back, and he's having a sup of whiskey at Breen's, so I thought I'd just come ahead and give you all the bend.

LIZZIE : I'm sure it's very kind of you, Tom. Oh! I wish Annie was here, or Helena—I haven't seen her all the morning either. I'd better get a cup of tea for him, anyway.

MOONEY : Don't bother about the tea, miss. Put him to bed the minute he comes in.

LIZZIE : Yes, that's a good idea.

MOONEY : And have a couple of hot water bottles ready.

LIZZIE : Yes.

MOONEY : And give him two aspirins.

LIZZIE : Two? Yes.

MOONEY : And tell the master I'll be back in a little while as soon as Master Eddie is dried off. I'm afraid there'll be a few questions I'll have to put to him.

LIZZIE (*fussing about the room*): What an upset it all is—poor Eddie—aspirin and hot-water bottles—where are my keys? Tom, do you see my keys anywhere?

MOONEY (*starting to look*) : What class of keys?

LIZZIE : Oh, just a bunch of keys. Oh, Eddie, Eddie! Mr. Hegarty, for goodness sake have a look round for a bunch of keys. (*They all start looking*). The kettle's sure to be off the boil—'twould be bound to happen. If Helena was her itself—

MOONEY : I have them here, miss, here on the writing table.

LIZZIE (*taking them*) Thank you, Tom. I won't be two minutes now. (*She goes out*).

HEGARTY : Is there any statement you'd like to make?

MOONEY : About what?

HEGARTY : Master Eddie.

MOONEY : Who the devil are you?

HEGARTY : I write for the papers, and—

MOONEY : Ah! go to blazes.

HEGARTY : There is nothing you want to say?

MOONEY : There is not.

HEGARTY : I see. It's a pity. It might have got your name before the public.

MOONEY : I don't want my name before the public. I want to live quiet. Here, out with you.

HEGARTY : Before I go I have a statement to make in connection with poisons.

MOONEY : I won't hear it. I'm bothered out of my life with people coming to me with statements about attempted murders and suicides and God knows what. I'll hear no more of them. (CHRISTINE *comes in, in evident distress*).

CHRISTINE : Is Eddie ——? Oh! I beg your pardon.

MOONEY : That all right, Miss Lambert. (*To* HEGARTY) Out of this, you.

HEGARTY : But really ——

MOONEY : No more talk. (*He pushes him out*) Master Eddie's as right as rain and will be here in a minute.

CHRISTINE : They told me at the factory he was drowned.

MOONEY : Wisha, bad luck to them for story-tellers.

CHRISTINE : Then in the street they said he had only got a ducking.

MOONEY : Let you sit down. You're all of a tremble.

CHRISTINE : Thank you, Mr. Mooney.

MOONEY (*moving to the door*) : I'll see that they send Eddie home; he should get out of his wet clothes and not be drinking at Breen's. (*He hesitates: he comes back to her*). Miss Lambert, if you'll excuse the intrusion, we've all a great respect for John Twohig and the family and I'd be sorry anything to happen Eddie.

CHRISTINE : Happen to Eddie? But he's safe, isn't he?

MOONEY : He is in one way, and he isn't in another. It'll be my business, I'm afraid, to find out what brought him into the water to-day, and, begging your pardon, it'll be a little bit your business too.

CHRISTINE (*getting up indignantly*) : I had nothing to do with it. What do you mean? What are you accusing me of?

MOONEY (*soothingly*) : Now, there's no use flying out at me. I'm too old, and I'm married; that makes me patient. Everyone in town knows you and Master Eddie. Everyone likes the two of you; and that's a sweet little place John has outside the town.

CHRISTINE : I don't know it.

MOONEY : 'Tis well you know it. The last time you were down here, didn't I see you and Eddie walking the land? Good land and a smart, tidy little garden all going to waste because John's too busy to live out there. A doaty little house—a woman living out there would be crowned. However, I won't go into all that. I'll just hint that, under certain circumstance (*Voice* EDDIE, *off*) I might overlook any charge I might have to bring against the young gentleman in question. I think I hear him coming. (*He goes to the door and looks out*). Come in here, Eddie, for a minute before you go to your room. There's someone wants to see you.

EDDIE (*heard off*) : Who is it?

MOONEY : 'Tis Miss Lambert.

EDDIE (*heard off*) : No, no, I can't come in.

MOONEY (*going outside the door*) : In with you and no nonsense. (*There is a bit of a scuffle outside and* MOONEY *shoots in* EDDIE. EDDIE *looks very woebegone: he has no hat and his hair is tousled and wet. Someone has lent him an overcoat old and too big for him. Below it are seen two wet flannel-trousered legs).* Here he is for you, Miss Lambert.

CHRISTINE (*rushing to him*) :   Eddie, darling.

MOONEY :   Exactly. (*He goes softly out*).

CHRISTINE :   My darling, what happened to you?

EDDIE (*rather sniffy*) :   Let me go, Christine. I'm not—I want to change, I'm dripping.

CHRISTINE :   I know, darling. But what happened?

EDDIE :   Oh, nothing.

CHRISTINE :   Nothing? Nonsense. What did you do?

EDDIE (*glibly*):   Well, I was on a rock and I got giddy and fell into the sea.

CHRISTINE :   That may be a good enough story to tell round the town but it's not good enough for me. (*Softly*) Won't you tell me, Eddie.

EDDIE (*sniffing*) :   I was so miserable, Christine.

CHRISTINE :   I know, darling.

EDDIE :   It didn't seem worth going on with.

CHRISTINE :   I know.

EDDIE :   And there seemed no hope things would ever come right.

CHRISTINE :   I know.

EDDIE :   So—so I tried to make an end of it all.

CHRISTINE :   My poor darling.

EDDIE :   I'm no good at living, Christine.

CHRISTINE :   Hush, hush.

EDDIE :   But if I'm no good at living, I'm as bad at dying. For the minute I felt the cold of the water I wanted to get out of it quick and go on living, and unfortunately I'm an awfully strong swimmer so—so I just swam ashore and—and that's all.

CHRISTINE :   Darling.

EDDIE :   Wasn't I the fool to try and destroy myself by drowning? I should have tried any other way but that.

CHRISTINE :   Darling. . . . . Eddie, do you know I've called you "darling" about a dozen times in the last two minutes?

EDDIE (*quite dumb*) :   Have you, Christine?

CHRISTINE :   Yes, darling.

EDDIE :   Well.

CHRISTINE :   Oh, you donkey.

EDDIE : You don't mean ———? Oh, Christine.

CHRISTINE (*in his arms*) : Of course I mean. If you'd been drowned, Eddie, I'd have been the next off that rock, and I can't swim. (ANNIE *appears.* *She is in outdoor clothes.* *She takes in the situation at a glance*).

ANNIE (*a little stern*) : Hm. Upstairs with you Eddie, and get out of your wet things.

EDDIE : Yes, Mammy. But Christine says she'll———

ANNIE : I think I know quite well what Christine says, but off with you . Do you want to get your death of cold?

EDDIE : No, mammy. Very well, mammy. I won't be five minutes changing, Christine.

ANNIE : You'll have a hot bath and you'll go to bed. Your Aunt Lizzie has everything ready for you.

EDDIE : Very well, mammy. But I'm not going to bed. (*He dashes out*).

ANNIE (*softening*) : I had to hunt him, Miss Lambert. I don't want him down on our hands with pneumonia.

CHRISTINE : Do you mind, Mrs. Twohig?

ANNIE : Mind?

CHRISTINE : Eddie and me———?

ANNIE : Sure my dear, it's what I've been wanting ever since I set eyes on you. Eddie's foolish in some ways and a bit young, but he's as good as gold and I know you'll make a fine man of him.

CHRISTINE : Eddie's splendid, Mrs. Twohig, splendid.

ANNIE : We'll talk it all out by and by. I've a lot of things on my mind this morning. You'll stay, won't you. It's not worth going back to the factory before dinner.

CHRISTINE : Yes, I'll stay. I'll just run upstairs and tidy myself. I rushed out of the factory without so much as a hat—and I think I've been crying.

ANNIE : Well, off with you. (CHRISTINE *goes out.* ANNIE *goes to the door and calls*). Helena. Helena! Bad luck to that girl; there's no getting any good out of her these days. (*She goes out. There is a little pause.* JOHN *comes in pushing* PETER *in front of him.* JOHN *looks very stern;* PETER *very frightened and small.* JOHN *locks the door*).

JOHN : Tell it to me again. I want to know are me ears mad or what.

PETER (*in a tiny voice*) : Well, 'twas an all-night sitting, as you know, and the Minister for Agriculture made a terrible powerful speech and——

JOHN : To hell with the Minister for Agriculture. Why did you listen to him?

PETER : I couldn't sort of help it. He made a terrible powerful speech and——

JOHN : And you let yourself be swayed by a bit of mob oratory?

PETER : It was not mob oratory, John, it was not. It was facts and figures and——

JOHN : Facts and figures. What the hell business have you with facts and figures? Your business is to vote with the Government.

PETER : I know. But——

JOHN : But?

PETER : It was that play, " An Enemy of the People "—do you remember it, John? I couldn't get it out of my head.

JOHN : Oh, those bloody plays.

PETER : Do you remember when the doctor in the play said that nobody should act so that he'd have to spit in his own face? I felt I sort of had to tell the truth, and the only way I could tell the truth—I'm no speechifier—was by my vote.

JOHN : So you voted against the Government?

PETER : I did.

JOHN : And defeated the bill?

PETER : Yes.

JOHN : And now the Government has to go to the country?
PETER : I suppose so.

JOHN : Suppose so? Don't you know? And don't you know that this place is disgraced for ever in the eyes of the world? Why, thunder and turf, man, what's going to become of public life at all if members of Parliament start being swayed this way and that by speeches and arguments, facts and figures, moryah? There's an end to all stability in public affairs; nobody will know where they stand; no party will know from day to day whether it has a majority or not; it's chaos, man, pure chaos.

PETER : I know, I know. I'll never do it again.

JOHN : You'll never have the chance to do it again, me bucko.

Do you think you're going to be candidate at the next election?

PETER : I suppose I won't.

JOHN : I know you won't.

PETER : It was that play—" An Enemy of the People."

JOHN : " An Enemy of the People." Faith, that's you; that's your name from this out.

PETER : I nearly cried in the car coming down—I got a lift as far as Shangarry Strand and I kem on by bus. I'm afraid to face the wife, though she herself was mad about that same play.

JOHN : Ah, don't talk to me about those plays, they have been the ruination of this place. However, thanks to Annie, I have already made up my mind how to deal with them. (*He goes to the door and unlocks it*). You'd better be off home, Peter, and get it over. We'll be friends again one of these days, but for the next week for God's sake keep out of my sight.

PETER (*meekly*) : Very well, John. (*He goes out*).

JOHN (*calling from the door*) : Annie. Annie.

ANNIE (*heard off*) : Yes, John.

JOHN : Come here. (ANNIE *comes in*). It's even worse than you thought.

ANNIE : What is?

JOHN : That play business. Peter Hurley's put out the Government on the head of some blasted play.

ANNIE : In heaven's name! That's awful, John.

JOHN : 'Tis a national tragedy—and to think that we're to blame for it all. Are they upstairs? Fetch them down. The sooner the whole thing is settled the better.

ANNIE : I think they're just after coming in from the Pavilion. I'll get them.

JOHN : Do so. And, Annie, come back yourself. You'll be a great help in case they turn nasty.

ANNIE : Very well. There's one thing, John . Eddie had a little accident this morning; he got a wetting. Say nothing to him about it, and if you hear any gossip in the town pay no heed to it.

JOHN : What do you mean? What's all this about?

ANNIE : Nothing at all. Pay no heed to anything but what I tell you. All's turned out for the best, and Eddie's going to marry

Miss Lambert.

JOHN : The devil he is. Well, I'm delighted. Me bold Eddie.

ANNIE : I knew you would be. I'll go call Mr. de la Mare. (*She goes out.* JOHN *sits at the writing table, takes out a cheque book and writes a cheque.* HECTOR *and* CONSTANCE *come in.* HECTOR *has a large envelope in his hand.* ANNIE *follows them*).

HECTOR : You wanted to see us, Mr. Twohig?

JOHN : I did. Will you sit down. (*The three sit.* JOHN *stands*). It's a bit hard for me to say what I have to say. Maybe I'd better begin by giving you this. (*He hands him the cheque*).

HECTOR (*looking at it*) : Fifty pounds? What is that for?

JOHN : Maybe you don't remember that it was in our agreement that the contract at the Pavilion could be terminated on either side without notice on payment of fifty pounds?

HECTOR : Oh. . . . . But—I do not understand. I admit that the audiences this week have been a disappointment, a sore disappointment, but I am confident that they will improve as the week goes on.

CONSTANCE : Miss Joyce bought three seats while we were there just now.

JOHN : It's got nothing to do with the audiences.

HECTOR : You can't have any complaint about the acting. I'm sure.

JOHN : I've nothing against the acting—'tis very good.

ANNIE : Too good.

HECTOR : Or the conduct of the company?

JOHN : No. Decent people, every one of them.

HECTOR : Then, I repeat, I do not understand.

JOHN : Well, it's this way. Queer things have started to happen here, things that never happened in fifty years, and it was Annie who put her finger on the root of the trouble.

CONSTANCE : What sort of things do you refer to, Mr. Twohig.

JOHN : You know very well, Miss Constance. Nasty things that were getting Inish into the paper.

CONSTANCE : And what have we to do with such things?

JOHN : Annie, maybe you could explain better than I can.

ANNIE : In a word, it's all you and your plays, Mr. de la Mare; and mind, I'm not saying a word against you personally or Miss Constantia either, but maybe they're too good for the like of us or we're too simple for them. I remember saying the morning you came—God forgive me—that we were blue-mouldy here for want of a good scandal or two; well, it seems there were lots of scandalous things going on in the town that no one knew anything of except the parties concerned. We were all more or less happy and comfortable, good tempered and jolly—until these plays began to put ideas into our heads. We got suspicious of our neighbours and of our own families. The young people got asking themselves " Is life worth living?" If I've heard that question asked once in the last week I've heard it asked a dozen times. My own boy asked it of me! Sure never before did we think of asking ourselves such a ridiculous question.

HECTOR : It is far from ridiculous, Mrs. Twohig. Is it worth living? I often wonder.

ANNIE : Ah, don't talk nonsense, man . Of course it is.

CONSTANCE : You have faith, Mrs. Twohig.

ANNIE : I have my religion, Miss Constantia. Did you ever see a big stone in a field, Mr. de la Mare?

HECTOR : Of course I did.

ANNIE : You might be sitting by it, idle-like, some sunny afternoon, and then for no reason at all you'd turn it over. And what would you see? Worms. Little beetles that'd run this way and that, horrible little creepies that'd make your stomach turn, and you'd put the stone back as quick as you could, or you'd run away.

HECTOR : I see, I see. A splendid simile, Mrs. Twohig. We have lifted the stone, we have exposed Inish. Constance, its wonderful. We have a mission here, a great duty.

JOHN : Oh no, sir, you haven't. Your duty is to get yourself and your traps out of the hall as quick as you can. Annie and myself saw the Monsignor early this morning and he agrees with the course I'm taking.

ANNIE : He agrees that there must be a stop put to people going into suicide pacts on the head of " Is life worth living?"

CONSTANCE : What nonsense. It shows great moral courage.

ANNIE : Whining and running away. A thing we never did before in Ireland.

HECTOR : You know you really can't turn us out like this at a moment's notice.

JOHN : The agreement says I can, and things is so desperate that I have to stick by that agreement even if it seems a bit hard on you. Do you know that we'd have a murder on our consciences only by the good luck that McCluskey the butcher is such a bad shot with a hatchet.

CONSTANCE : I don't believe that had anything to do with our plays.

JOHN : And Tommy McCluskey in the front row every night. Of course, we all knew he fought now and again with Julia, but the night he threw the hatchet was the night he came home after seeing Mr. de la Mare throw the lamp at you.

HECTOR : But there are quite a number of seats booked for to-night, Mr. Twohig. Are you going to disappoint those people?

JOHN (*with a confident smile*) : They'll get their money's worth.

HECTOR : In what way?

JOHN : I was on the 'phone this morning to Shangarry Strand. I'm having the circus over.

HECTOR (*really pained*) : A circus!

JOHN : It's on the road now. It will be in the town any minute.

CONSTANCE (*outraged*) : This is an insult, a deliberate insult.

JOHN : It's nothing of the kind.

CONSTANCE : You are a narrow, bigoted man; you are afraid of the truth, and your wife is worse; she is an ignorant provincial. She has only seen our work twice——

ANNIE : Twice was enough.

CONSTANCE : We were giving you great art. I have player here as I have never played before. Mr. de la Mare has given himself—all of himself—night after night to an audience of—clodhoppers. And now, when we stir something in these clods, waken them to some spark of life, you say they must go to sleep again, and you rock them to sleep with a circus. It's an insult to them and to us.

ANNIE : I don't know what you mean by awakening them to life, Miss Constantia. It seems to me you were awakening them to kill each other or themselves, and to say mean slanderous things of each other and——

JOHN : And to put out the Government. Oh! when I think of that Peter Hurley——

ANNIE : The long and the short of it is, you were doing no good here and you must be gone.

HECTOR : You really mean this?

JOHN : I do.

HECTOR : I can only say that I am sorry. I think you are mistaken—tragically mistaken—in your attitude, but you have treated us fairly all along and I am not going to stoop to a sordid quarrel. (*He puts the cheque in his pocket*). My wife has said some things she should not have said, but I know that you'll forgive her.

ANNIE : Of course. Sure, dear, I'm sorry for you.

CONSTANCE (*sitting down and crying a little*) : We were so happy here; you were all so kind to us, I thought we were fixed for the whole summer. I'm so tired of dragging from place to place.

ANNIE (*going to her with lovely sympathy*) : I know, dear, I know. But you mustn't think of going away, not until you've settled where you can go. This is your home for as long as you care to stay. Isn't that so, John.

JOHN : To be sure it is. I'll take it badly if you go away in a huff.

CONSTANCE (*sniffing*) : Thank you, Mrs. Twohig.

HECTOR : I appreciate your attitude Mrs. Twohig, and I am very grateful for your offer of hospitality. We shall probably avail ourselves of it for a few days. I think it will be only for a few days, because our success here has had reverbations elsewhere and I have at least two very good offers in my pocket.

JOHN : I'm more than delighted to hear that.

HECTOR : Let us go to the Pavilion, darling, and start to pack.

CONSTANCE (*rising*) : Very well. (*As they reach the door* CONSTANCE *whispers something to* HECTOR).

HECTOR : Oh, yes . . . Mrs. Twohig, if that young newspaper man comes back you might give him this envelope; it contains some photographs he particularly asked for.

ANNIE (*taking the envelope*) : Certainly.

HECTOR (*to* JOHN) : And keep a couple of seats for us to-night, please; it's twenty years since I've seen a circus. (*They go out*).

JOHN : Well, that's over. They took it very nicely.

ANNIE : They did, the creatures.

JOHN (*crossing to the sideboard*) :   I think I deserve a little drink after that.

ANNIE :   You do, to be sure.

JOHN :   You ought to make a cup of tea for yourself.

ANNIE :   I'll have a glass of port instead.

JOHN (*astonished*) :   Annie, what's come to you?

ANNIE :   I don't know, but I feel so light in the heart, as if a big cloud was gone.

JOHN :   Faith, you're welcome to a bucket of port, but here's a wineglassful to begin with. (*As he is pouring it out* HELENA *comes in. She is in outdoor clothes*).

ANNIE :   Helena, where were you?   I was looking everywhere for you.

HELENA :   I know, ma'am.   I was at the chapel, ma'am.

ANNIE :   And what were you doing at the chapel this hour of the morning.

HELENA :   I was getting married, ma'am.

ANNIE :   Merciful heaven!   Who to?

HELENA :   Michael, of course.   Who else?

ANNIE :   Oh, my poor girl, is this what has come of all that nasty talk?   Why didn't you tell me?   I'd have told you not to mind a thing they said and not to tie yourself up for life with a man who's no more to you than the next.

HELENA :   It's not that way at all, ma'am.   Michael and me have been promised to each other for the last two months, only I never could bring myself to tell him about—you know what.   I was delighted it slipped out of me that morning.   Anyway, to stop tongues wagging, we thought we might as well be married at once.

Warn Band off (Record).

JOHN :   Well, thunder and turf!   That's one good thing the plays did, anyhow.   Where's Michael?   (*Start record*).

HELENA :   Outside the door, listening. (*Raising her voice*) You can come in, Michael, they're not mad at all. (MICHAEL *comes in a little sheepish*).   (*Band*).

JOHN :   Oh, there's the bold bridegroom.   Hold up your head, Michael.   Here, put the hand there and I wish you the best of luck.

MICHAEL :   Thank you, sir.

ANNIE : And I wish you the same, and the best of luck to you, Helena, and years of happiness.

HELENA : Thank you, ma'am, you've always been the good friend to me. (LIZZIE *hurries in*).

LIZZIE : A band, John, a band.

ANNIE : Where?

LIZZIE : Coming up the street, I think. I heard it from the upper window.

JOHN (*cooly*) : Did you ever hear of a circus without a band?

LIZZIE
HELENA   } : A circus?
MICHAEL

JOHN : In the Pavilion to-night, and free seats for all the town. (*Music is heard*).

HELENA : Glory.

MICHAEL : I hear the band myself. Come out to the door, Helena. (*He and* HELENA *rush out*).

LIZZIE : And look, there's the sun bursting out.

ANNIE : My heart's leppin with joy.

(*It is quite true; the room is flooded with sunshine.* CHRISTINE *and* EDDIE *rush in and make for the window.* EDDIE *is dressed in his nicest suit*).

EDDIE : A band, Pappy, a band.

CHRISTINE : Eddie, am I mad or do I see a clown?

LIZZIE (*crowding to the window*) : A clown? Clowns are my joy.

EDDIE (*with a shout*) : Two clowns.

CHRISTINE (*topping him*) : Three.

LIZZIE : And a doaty little girl in spangles on a piebald pony. John, what's the meaning of it all?

JOHN : We've put back the old stone, Lizzie, thank God.

ANNIE : Amen.

LIZZIE : I don't know what you mean. Anyhow, it sounds grand. (*The music has swelled nearer. The band is playing "Stars and Stripes For Ever."*)

(EDDIE *and* CHRISTINE *can't resist it. They must do a little dance together in the background.* LIZZIE *staring out the window is softly clapping her hands and smiling.* JOHN *and* ANNIE *are near the front*).

JOHN : Annie, get on the telephone to Dublin.

ANNIE : Why so?

JOHN : Get on to the best shop in the city. I think I owe you a new dress.

ANNIE : Maybe you do . . . . . have you got six coppers? (*He fingers for them. The music fills the room*).

THE CURTAIN FALLS

THE   END.

LMP
PL7400
LTA   P